Praise

Amy and Embrace Grace have landed on a model that loves women and their babies in their most intense moments of need. Amy's example of compassion toward these most vulnerable individuals is an inspiration for our movement as we strive to always love them both.

LILA ROSE
Founder and president of Live Action; host of *The Lila Rose Show* podcast

Amy Ford truly lives out the gospel through her love and compassionate care of women experiencing unplanned pregnancies. *Help Her Be Brave* is so inspiring and a great guide on how we can support, encourage, and empower new mothers.

PATRICIA HEATON
Emmy Award winning actress

Abortion is a topic of frequent discussion on *Joni Table Talk*, and as I think of the beauty of those children with Jesus, I also feel the hurt of the many women who have made that choice. In *Help Her Be Brave*, Amy Ford not only reveals her own trauma but provides practical steps to reach out to abortion-vulnerable women. A must-read, especially for church leaders.

JONI LAMB
Cofounder, Daystar Television Network

Amy is brave in her conviction that we can all help moms to be brave enough to say yes to God in their pregnancy. Amy unpacks simple yet profound ways all of us can help make the difference between life and death, the temporary and eternity. She walks what she talks and shows us all how we can too.

JOR-EL GODSEY
Heartbeat International

Amy Ford's unwavering commitment to the pro-life movement is inspiring. Her message hits close to home, as my mother considered aborting me after she was raped. Women need someone to come alongside them after an unexpected pregnancy, and Amy has done that for many years through her organization Embrace Grace. "The life decisions we witness and the glory stories we hear become the fuel that keeps us dedicated to the cause," she writes. The extensive list of ideas and resources she provides will give readers the tools they need to be God's love in action and take a stand for what truly matters.

JAMES ROBISON
Founder and president, LIFE Outreach International

Wow Amy! You rock! You are so right! Come on church, we need to Embrace Grace (God's grace) and help her to be brave. I was single and pregnant at sixteen years old. I had no one to talk to and I chose abortion for my baby, a decision that I will regret and struggle with the rest of my life. But we (the church) have the power to stand in the gap with girls like me, like Amy, like so many out there. They don't need a lecture but they need God's love and our grace! Let's be the face of Jesus for these ashamed, afraid, and often abused women! Let's work together to save mommies who save their babies! Amy has the guide right here! Pick it up, read it, and act on it. Lives depend on it!

LISA ROBERTSON
Author and speaker

Amy's passion to help young women with unplanned pregnancies comes through each page of this book, beginning with her very vulnerable and personal story. What God has done through Amy and Embrace Grace is nothing short of amazing! I hope that every pastor and leader reads this book about how a pro-love movement—that began as a small group and has now swept the nation and the world—is calling the church to not only save babies of unplanned pregnancies but to also provide the moms of those babies with the support and love that they need.

ROBERT MORRIS
Senior Pastor, Gateway Church; bestselling author of *The Blessed Life*, *Beyond Blessed*, and *Take the Day Off*

One of the main reasons that women choose abortion is fear. They fear the father of the baby will abandon them. They fear rejection by their families. They fear their unknown future. But God's Word reminds us that perfect love casts out fear. This is a truth that Amy Ford knows well and lives well. Indeed, she is the embodiment of what it means to be "pro-love" and her fantastic book will inspire you to be "pro-love" too.

ROLAND C. WARREN
President and CEO of Care Net; author of *Bad Dads of the Bible: 8 Mistakes Every Good Dad Can Avoid*

One of the most important elements before I get on stage is the master of ceremonies. Amy is one of the greatest MCs I have ever met because she sets the stage for children who aren't even here yet.

MICHAEL JR.
Comedian

Amy is a pro-life powerhouse who draws you in with eye-opening stories, including her own, and then engages you further to identify impactful ways to get involved in the pro-life community. It's the perfect balance of storytelling paired with a wide range of tangible ways to love women well who are experiencing unexpected pregnancies. Church, it's time to rise up, and Amy's ready to show us how!

ABBY JOHNSON
Founder, And Then There Were None; pro-life activist and author

HELP
HER BE
BRAVE

DISCOVERING YOUR PLACE IN THE
PRO-LIFE MOVEMENT

AMY FORD

MOODY PUBLISHERS
CHICAGO

© 2021 by
AMY FORD

Edited by Annette LaPlaca
Interior Design: Erik M. Peterson
Cover design and illustration by Brooklynn West
Author photo: Meshali Mitchell

Library of Congress Cataloging-in-Publication Data

Names: Ford, Amy, author.
Title: Help her be brave : discover your place in the pro-life movement /
  Amy Ford.
Description: Chicago : Moody Publishers, [2020] | Includes bibliographical
  references. | Summary: "What if we lived in a world where every woman
  with an unplanned pregnancy always felt empowered to choose life for her
  unborn baby? With Help Her Be Brave, you can discover your part in
  saving lives and find your pro-life passion"-- Provided by publisher.
Identifiers: LCCN 2020034744 (print) | LCCN 2020034745 (ebook) | ISBN
  9780802423115 (paperback) | ISBN 9780802499509 (ebook)
Subjects: LCSH: Abortion--Moral and ethical aspects. | Right to life. |
  Pro-life movement.
Classification: LCC HQ767.15 .F67 2020 (print) | LCC HQ767.15 (ebook) |
  DDC 179.7/6--dc23
LC record available at https://lccn.loc.gov/2020034744
LC ebook record available at https://lccn.loc.gov/2020034745

Originally delivered by fleets of horse-drawn wagons, the affordable paperbacks from D. L. Moody's publishing house resourced the church and served everyday people. Now, after more than 125 years of publishing and ministry, Moody Publishers' mission remains the same— even if our delivery systems have changed a bit. For more information on other books (and resources) created from a biblical perspective, go to www.moodypublishers.com or write to:

Moody Publishers
820 N. LaSalle Boulevard
Chicago, IL 60610

1 3 5 7 9 10 8 6 4 2

Printed in the United States of America

For Ryan,
who continues to cheer me on and challenge me.
You make everything better.

For Jess and Audrey, Mackenzie, Landry, and Judah,
I love you guys so much.
You are all world changers.

For the Pro-Life and Pro-Love Warriors,
thank you for giving all you have to save lives.
We are better together.

CONTENTS

Foreword   9

Introduction   11

1. **See Her**
   Finding the Ones Who Need Us   21

2. **Comfort Her**
   Partnering with Pregnancy Centers   37

3. **Welcome Her**
   Opening the Doors to Community   53

4. **Protect Her**
   Speaking Up for the Powerless   73

5. **Love Her**
   Creating a Safe Place for Inner Healing   91

6. **Support Her**
   Being There for the Ones Who Choose Adoption   107

7. **Free Her**
   Breaking Your Chains So Others Can Break Theirs   129

8. **Empower Her**
   Ending the Cycle of Poverty   143

9. **Know Her**
   Paving the Way for Pure Hearts   169

10. **Embrace Her**
    Inviting Others to Join the Kingdom   185

Beauty for Ashes   199

Acknowledgments   203

Notes   205

FOREWORD

The 1973 decision in *Roe v. Wade* marked a devastating shift in our country as the Supreme Court legalized abortion. Since that ruling, over 60 million babies have been lost to abortion in the US. Those of us who believe life is sacred—and that it begins at the moment of conception—grieve over this staggering loss of preborn life. I can't help but wonder how many frightened women might have made a different choice if they'd been offered the kind of empowering support that Amy Ford lays out in this book.

For far too many women facing unplanned pregnancies, abortion feels like the only option. Our team at Focus hears from expectant mothers on a regular basis who express shock, fear, and shame as the news of their pregnancies sinks in. They wonder what their church and family will say, how they'll afford to raise a child, and what their future will hold if they move forward with their pregnancy. Others contact us to express their deep regret over past abortions.

And then there are the women who tell us they came within days, hours, or even moments of seeking an abortion, only to choose life in the eleventh hour. Whether they made the decision to parent their babies or place them for adoption, time and again we read letters and emails describing the gratitude and relief these courageous women have experienced in the wake of that momentous choice.

This begs the question: What will it take to see more women make this life-giving decision? How can we foster a culture in which abortion becomes unthinkable, and every tiny life in the womb is cherished and protected? What are some practical things we can do to come alongside expectant moms with Christlike compassion, tangible assistance, and the truth of God's tender love and care for them and their babies?

Amy answers all of these questions and more as she urges the church to be a safe haven for pregnant women. Her passion to see believers reach out to vulnerable women and their babies is contagious, and I pray many of our fellow Christians will catch Amy's inspiring vision.

With great sensitivity and insight into the plight of women facing unplanned pregnancies, Amy holds a mirror up to the Christian community, powerfully challenging us to rally around the hurting and needy people in our midst. She shares her heart for ministering to "the least of these" and shows us what it looks like—on a practical, day-to-day basis—to extend love and support to those desperately seeking hope amidst a surprise pregnancy.

Amy reminds us not just that each preborn baby has incalculable value, but that so, too, does every mother-to-be. Regardless of how a woman finds herself expecting, she is loved beyond measure by the God who created her—and, thus, she is worthy of care, respect, and dignity.

May we be a people who give a cup of cold water to anyone thirsting for refreshment. May we seek out those who need a helping hand. And when we cross paths with an overwhelmed woman who has discovered she carries a precious little one in her womb, may we go above and beyond to help her be brave.

JIM DALY | President, Focus on the Family

INTRODUCTION

C ould I really go through with this?

I barely registered the words of the nurses who were fanning me. I was coming around after having fainted in a doctor's office, and I could not stop weeping.

"You shouldn't have a procedure today. You're too emotionally distraught." They sent me away with instructions to reschedule.

By the time I reached my boyfriend, Ryan, in the waiting room, I knew I wasn't going to have an abortion. *Looks like we're really going to do this. I'm having a baby.*

I thank God for that nurse who told me, "Today you're not getting an abortion." But that's how close we came to never knowing our beautiful, wonderful, God-given son Jess.

At nineteen years old, I nearly chose abortion out of *fear*—fear for how it would completely change all the plans I had for my life and all the plans Ryan had for his, fear of disappointing my family and my church, fear of how it would change all my friendships, and more. Many girls or young women finding themselves with an unplanned pregnancy share these same fears—and so many more: fear of abandonment and being completely alone, fear of emotionally or physically abusive boyfriends or family members, fear of not being able to afford anything for herself much less for herself and a child too. For a single and pregnant woman, the future can be absolutely *terrifying*.

All the plans Ryan and I had for our lives *were* changed forever—but God, who loves us so much, gave us a hope and a beautiful future even better than what we'd imagined. My family and friends *were* hurt and disappointed, but not only did they not reject me, they immediately prepared, even with joyful anticipation, to love Ryan and our baby for keeps. My pregnancy *did* affect my friendships, but I couldn't know then how God would bless my life with years and years of deep, meaningful friendships and ministry with women He brought into my life.

When faced with that unplanned pregnancy at age nineteen, I needed to be brave. I thank God I had Ryan and our families, friends, and faith community to help me be brave. It's obvious why I am now so wholeheartedly pro-life—*pro-love!* And it was just like God to use every event of my life—even the parts that were the hardest or came from my own foolish actions—to equip me to help other women be brave.

When God gave me the idea to invite women with unplanned pregnancies into a small group at church in order to shower them with love, I pitched the idea to my small groups pastor and she told me to run with it. She loved the idea. I felt nervous and under-qualified to begin a group like that, but I knew it was what I should do.

My friend Salina joined me in the project, and we spent a summer preparing before our first group launched. We prayed about a name and concluded that *Embrace Grace* would be appropriate for the group. Our hope was that mommas would embrace grace for themselves and the church would embrace grace for the mommas. At the time, there was no such thing as a "single and pregnant" curriculum so we had to improvise. We searched for "Embrace Grace" on the Internet to see what would come up. We were drawn to a book by Liz Curtis Higgs entitled *Embrace Grace*. It wasn't about unplanned pregnancies, but it focused on God's grace and love for us. It was perfect. We planned to use it as the core study for the group.

That fall, three mommas showed up to the first class. All three seemed defeated and scared for their future. They wouldn't make much eye contact, and their shoulders seemed to sag. We could almost smell the hopelessness when they walked into the room. One of the moms wore a coat around her to make her pregnancy less visible (and it was August . . . in Texas). Our mission became clearer by the minute. These young women needed to embrace grace and be embraced *by* grace.

For twelve weeks, we shared the hope of Jesus. We laughed together and cried together. We were vulnerable with each other. We replaced the enemy's lies with God's truth. In every way we knew how, we empowered these mommas to be the mothers God created them to be.

By the end of the semester, all three seemed like completely different women. They stood tall and confident. Their shoulders were squared, and they looked as if a five-hundred-pound burden had been lifted. There was a new sparkle in their eyes. They were ready. Whatever was coming, whatever God had in store, they trusted Him to take care of them and their babies. They were so *brave*.

Love had transformed them.

As leaders, we were in awe of what God had done in such a short time. We launched a new semester, and three more moms came, then eighteen, then twenty-one, then thirty-six. Eventually, other churches started asking for information about how they could start a group at their church. Over time we started writing a curriculum focused on identity and worth found in Jesus.

Before long, Embrace Grace was blessing mommas we had never met as baby showers and support groups spread from city to city. Salina and I looked at each other in wonder. God was building something much bigger than one small group at Gateway Church, and we knew it. He was starting a movement of love among believers that would travel beyond cities and spread from nation to nation. Through Embrace Grace, He wanted us to encourage the global church to be a refuge for the broken hearts of single and pregnant women. We believed He wanted us to turn what had begun as a small group for three discouraged women into a nonprofit organization that could inspire and equip churches all over the world.

People *are* the church. The church isn't a building. We are the church wherever we go, and we represent Jesus wherever we are. The church can play a powerful role in saving lives. It can help prevent unplanned pregnancies by affirming identity and the value of individuals as daughters and sons of a King and by talking about hard topics like sex and abstinence. The church can be one of the first places a girl runs to when she finds out she has an unplanned pregnancy. It should never be the place she avoids because of shame and guilt. The church can help her be brave and choose life. The church can reach out and invite these women and men into a spiritual family. The church can help heal past hurts and wounds because free people *free* people. The church can help practically by giving single or struggling moms support so they don't just survive, they thrive.

If abortion became illegal today, the church wouldn't be ready.

Most Christians *say* they want to live that way. But I believe the same Christians who have taken a stance for the sanctity of life don't realize that *if abortion became illegal today, the church wouldn't be ready.*

What would we do if there were women who were pregnant and scared, even angry, that they must carry an unplanned baby to term? It wouldn't be right for us to look away and say, "Good luck!" We would have to be available to assist spiritually, emotionally, and physically.

It's time to get the church ready. We can't ignore these mommas anymore.

We can't ignore the statistics, either:

- 40% of all births are to unmarried women[1]
- 18% of all U.S. pregnancies ended in abortion in 2017[2]
- 85.2% of all abortions in 2013 were with unmarried women[3]
- 4 in 10 women who have had abortions were attending church regularly at the time of their abortion decision[4]

- Approximately 11 million children under the age of 18 are raised by single parents[5]

I was almost one of those statistics. Yes, I almost chose abortion because I was terrified to tell my parents. But fear of telling her loved ones is not the only reason a woman considers terminating a pregnancy.

According to Guttmacher,[6] the top reasons why women choose an abortion are

- Having a child would interfere with a woman's education, work, or ability to care for dependents
- The woman/family can't afford a baby right now
- Single motherhood or relationship problems

Whatever the reasons a woman might seek an abortion, all of them are rooted in fear. My friend Destiny, who had an unplanned pregnancy as a teen, said it best, "See, you don't realize how temporary the 'crisis' is when it's consuming your every waking moment, but as soon as you get beyond that . . . Such beauty can be born from that which we never planned. Fear is temporary, but the courage you gain facing it lasts forever. Panic subsides, but the strength you find in the midst of the crisis endures. Perhaps the most amazing thing, though, is how the love you feel for this new life, whether it was intended or not, suddenly turns a 'mistake' into a miracle. I didn't save my son by 'choosing life.' He saved me."[7]

Young women like Destiny should not have to face an unplanned pregnancy alone. Together, we can eliminate her fears and help her be brave. How can we do it? The recipe for transforming fear to faith is simple. There is just one ingredient: love. First John 4:18 explains clearly, "There is no fear in love. But perfect love drives out fear, because fear has to do with punishment."

Love saves lives.

We punish women with unplanned pregnancies when we label them or ignore them. But it is not guilt that brings transformation. Only "the goodness of God leads [us] to repentance" (Rom. 2:4 NKJV). If we're not showing the goodness and kindness of our heavenly Father, how will anyone know the hope of Jesus? It is love alone that changes hearts and mindsets.

Simply put, love saves lives.

We can't just vote a certain way or talk about what needs to change, we *are* the change. And it will take all of us to create change. Miracles won't happen if we are content to pass by on the other side of the road when we see people who are hurting, bruised, and afraid. It is time to activate our beliefs by being "good Samaritans," bandaging the wounds of the broken and introducing them to the Healer of hearts.

Many of you may ask, "Okay, we need to love. But *how*? What does it look like in practical terms? How do I know where to start? Where do I find a place to serve or get involved? I don't even know what's out there or what I might have to offer."

I felt the same way a few years ago. I didn't even know there was a pro-life movement before I started Embrace Grace. After my first book, *A Bump in Life,* released, I received invitations to speak for various organizations. One of them was a Care Net

Conference, a training conference for pregnancy center workers. When I arrived at the conference, I saw hundreds of pro-life ministries lining the hotel hallways to share information about a service or life-saving ministry where people could connect and get involved. I walked up and down those halls in awe of the many amazing resources that were available. I kept thinking, *If only people knew about all these resources!*

The pro-life movement is filled with love and opportunity. The possibilities are endless. Whether you partner with an organization that is already doing great things or start something new on your own, there is a place for you to help and serve. God has put certain strengths, gifts, talents, and passions within you so you can use them to change the world. There is something unique inside you that equips you to help unlike any other person.

Here are a few questions to ask yourself as you pray about where to get involved:

1. What are you passionate about? What is your favorite hobby or thing to do in your spare time? Can it somehow connect to the pro-life movement? For example, if you love numbers and accounting, you might help a single mom create a budget. If you're familiar with human resources or love career coaching, you might help a single mom create her resume and find a good job. If you love children, you could offer to babysit. If you have a knack for fixing cars, you could help repair a single mom's car.

2. What makes you pound your fist on the table and say, "Someone needs to do something about this!"? That *some-*

one might be you. There's a reason why you get fired up about a certain injustice or cause.

3. What is your story? A lot of times, our purpose is tied to our story. Have you experienced an abortion and want to help others experience God's healing the way you have? Did an unplanned pregnancy leave you feeling completely alone? Perhaps you can be the person you wish had been there for you. God often uses our deepest pain as the launching pad for our greatest calling.

Look out into the world and see what breaks your heart. Run *toward* your heartbreak, not away from it. Dig in and ask God if your heart is broken because His is too. When your heartbreak becomes a map to find a place to serve, it will set your soul on fire. If all of us work together, we will make abortion unthinkable and empower women to be brave. We would be blessing future generations because brave moms raise brave kids!

This book is not intended to be a comprehensive directory of all the places to serve or all the ways you can help. But you may read something here that stirs your soul and compels you to act. Have an open heart, and just *start*. Take a step and see where the pro-love path leads; God may show you an opportunity you never knew to look for. You are a miracle waiting to happen. You are the answer to someone's prayer. There is a new mother out there who needs you. We can't fix all of her problems, but we can point her to the One who can.

Recently I was working the Embrace Grace booth at a pro-life women's conference and met a young woman named Terrisa, the founder and executive director of Pro-Life San Francisco. She leads a millennial-focused, grassroots activist group operating in arguably the most pro-choice city in America. She speaks to pro-life groups about secular and millennial outreach throughout the United States.

But what really makes Terrisa stand out in the pro-life community is that she is an atheist.

"Amy," she said when she walked up to the Embrace Grace booth, "I wanted to see if you would be one of the speakers at our upcoming Pro-Life San Francisco event that will take place at UC Berkeley. Would you be interested?"

I couldn't hide my surprise. "Ummm . . . you know what my message is about, right? The church, life, love—and Jesus. Wouldn't that be an issue for you?"

"Yeah, I know what your pro-love message is about. I don't believe in your God. But I believe in the power of your people. If you can get the church to actually *do something*, then the abortion issue wouldn't even be an issue. The pro-life side has the manpower because we have the church. We have got to activate the church to get involved, and things will start to change."

Whoa.

An atheist can recognize the power within us, but we haven't. Come on, Church! If we join together, using all the strengths and gifts God put inside each of us, we would push the tipping point back toward life.

And back toward love.

SEE HER

Finding the Ones Who Need Us

When I was nineteen, I was pregnant and unmarried. The shame and guilt were crippling. Growing up in church, I knew I was meant to save sex until marriage, but I still messed up. My boyfriend and I loved each other so much, and we had begun looking to each other for validation instead of to God.

I knew abortion was wrong. Even as a child I would prayerfully march outside abortion clinics with my family. If anyone ever asked me about that topic, I would adamantly say I could not understand why someone would choose abortion. But when I found out I was pregnant, fear took the wheel. I convinced myself an abortion would be the easy way out. Ryan and I would never have to tell a soul; we would never have to disappoint our families. Our plan was to pretend this little "bump in life" never happened and just keep going to church every Sunday.

Everything would be just fine.

I came within moments of having an abortion, having made it as far as being in a medical gown and sitting on the cold table. While the nurses were describing the way they would perform the abortion and what was about to happen, I had an anxiety attack, hyperventilated, and passed out.

Then, as the nurses were fanning me and trying to get me to drink some water, one of them looked me in the eyes and said, "You're too emotionally distraught to make this decision today. You can come back another day, but today you're not getting an abortion."

I walked back into the waiting room, and Ryan saw that my eyes were red and my face was swollen from crying so much.

"We're still pregnant," I said.

In that moment, we decided to just see what would happen. We were nervous about our future and about how our families would respond to the news. But we were determined to figure it out together and brace ourselves for the hard months ahead.

We were so close to losing our precious son because of fear, because of isolation, because of shame and feeling that no one would understand.

We were so close.

I no longer speak about the abortion debate as I did before. My thoughts haven't changed; I still know it's wrong. But now instead of talking about abortion dogmatically, I address it with compassion and empathy. My heart breaks for every momma considering abortion, knowing all the emotions and fears overwhelming her.

I married the father of my son when I was sixteen weeks pregnant. I always loved him and knew He was God's best for me, but our marriage didn't begin in the picture-perfect way I'd always dreamed. Shame intensified when we were planning the wedding. Ryan really wanted his mentor, the pastor who had helped introduce him to the Lord years before, to marry us. This pastor lived several hours away, but he and Ryan were still close friends. Ryan looked up to him and respected every word that came out of his mouth. He wanted to honor this dear mentor by inviting him to join us together as husband and wife.

I remember the shock when Ryan shared the pastor's response. Disappointment washed over his face, as he looked at the ground and said, "Well, he declined the invitation to marry us. He said we had sinned so he could not bless the marriage or marry us."

Our first church wound happened in that moment, and it wouldn't be the last. Rejection after rejection crept into our hearts, and the shame became unbearable. We believed we had messed up so badly we couldn't even get married and be blessed by God.

Finally, we found another amazing pastor to marry us, and I tried my best to suck in my belly as I walked down the aisle. It was hard to maintain happy thoughts on my wedding day when I kept wondering who knew about our pregnancy and thinking about how disappointed they must be. *Things will get better after we are married*, I repeated to myself. *Things will get better, things will get better . . .*

But they didn't.

The burden of shame made it hard for me to walk out of my apartment every day. The ache of rejection kept me from celebrating the life and miracle growing inside me. Though I was around people frequently, I still felt completely alone.

One by one, all my friends left. Looking back, I realize now that this wasn't because they didn't like me. They just didn't know what to do. Our pregnancy was "the elephant in the room." People didn't know whether to say, "Congratulations" or "I'm sorry." In the end, they didn't say anything at all.

Before getting pregnant I was active in the church and had a lot of friends there. After getting pregnant, I tried going back to church, but things had changed. No one acknowledged the pregnancy and the baby growing inside me. It was as if they couldn't see me. For some, it was hard to make eye contact. I felt invisible.

So I left.

Ryan and I did not go back to church until five or six years later. I tried different congregations but didn't find the perfect fit until I came to Gateway Church in Southlake, Texas. My family and I became involved right away. I began to feel God healing my heart. An unexpected part of that healing came when we got a phone call from an old friend.

The pastor who wouldn't marry us called my husband and asked for forgiveness. He said it was the worst mistake he'd ever made in his pastoring years. Of course Ryan forgave him. In fact, their relationship is a testimony to the healing power of love. They remain best friends to this day.

A few years ago, this same pastor asked me to come speak at his church on Mother's Day. He told me he had been prepping his congregation for a few weeks before I came. He had been very honest with them and told them how years ago he had refused to marry us. He confessed that he'd had a Pharisee heart at the time.

On that Mother's Day, I shared my deep convictions about how God's grace changes people. After my message, the pastor asked me to stay up on the platform, and he also called up my first-born son. In front of the entire congregation he said, "Amy, years ago I asked your husband for forgiveness for what I did. Now I'm asking *you*. Will you forgive me?"

Through tears, I said yes.

Then he turned to my teenaged son and said, "Jess, will you forgive me for planting seeds of rejection in your heart before you were even born? While you were still in your mother's womb, I rejected you. I am so sorry. Will you forgive me?"

Jess forgave him, too.

It was a powerful moment of freedom. Throughout the room, people were crying, as God healed old church wounds in many hearts. Everyone was changed in some way that day. God can restore broken relationships. But I still wish someone had reached out in love and acceptance years before.

WHAT THE BIBLE HAS TO SAY
ABOUT FINDING THE ONES WHO NEED US

Cathy was leading her first Embrace Grace group. She was excited, and her team had spent months dreaming and planning for the group of women who would be attending. The first day of class finally arrived, and to her surprise, only *one* mom showed up.

For a few more weeks, she held out hope that others would join, but no one else came.

Cathy was sharing her disappointment with God one morning,

and she heard the Lord say, "Cathy, would you do it all for just the one?" She realized she needed to see this situation through the eyes of her heavenly Father.

In Luke 15:1–7, we read,

> Now the tax collectors and sinners were all gathering around to hear Jesus. But the Pharisees and the teachers of the law muttered, "This man welcomes sinners and eats with them."
>
> Then Jesus told them this parable: "Suppose one of you has a hundred sheep and loses one of them. Doesn't he leave the ninety-nine in the open country and go after the lost sheep until he finds it? And when he finds it, he joyfully puts it on his shoulders and goes home. Then he calls his friends and neighbors together and says, 'Rejoice with me; I have found my lost sheep.' I tell you that in the same way there will be more rejoicing in heaven over one sinner who repents than over ninety-nine righteous persons who do not need to repent."

Don't miss how Jesus uses the word *until* in this passage. He doesn't say He goes after the lost sheep *until* he gets tired or *until* it gets dark. The Shepherd goes after the one "until he finds it." And He doesn't come back annoyed with the sheep or frustrated from the search, either. He comes back rejoicing, ready to celebrate that the lost one was found.

Christ's mission on earth was, and still is, to seek and to save that which is lost. He would gladly leave the ninety-nine to go after the one. The same search-and-rescue assignment has been given to us. We are to be actively looking for the wandering, the weak, and the weary. The Good Shepherd wants us to step out of our comfort zones to bring the lost back home.

DISCOVERING YOUR PLACE

As God's search-and-rescue team, the church waits expectantly for the Holy Spirit to guide us. Sometimes we overcomplicate the mission, questioning whether that still, small voice that prompts us to reach out is just a thought of our own. Too many times, we have missed moments when God was tugging on our heartstrings to look for the lonely.

Some of the thoughts we might have are, "The weather is not cooperating; I'll just pray at home instead of out on the sidewalk at an abortion clinic today." Or maybe if we hear of someone in our circle who has a son or daughter experiencing an unplanned pregnancy, we think, "I wanted to respect their privacy and not embarrass them by reaching out." Or maybe the Lord leads us to speak a kind word to a stranger who appears to be pregnant and not wearing a wedding ring, but we talk ourselves out of it because we worry it might come across as judgmental to ask.

So many times women will say, "God, give me a big sign." We can be the sign!

How odd that we wait for a divine moment to happen when God Himself lives in us. With God's Spirit enabling us, *every* moment can be a divine moment.

So many times women with an unintended pregnancy will

say, "There is no way I can have this baby. I told God, 'If You don't want me to go through with this abortion, then I need you to give me a big sign so I know You are going to help me. Otherwise, I'm going through with my appointment.'" This is a common thought process for women who are scared about their future. But we can be the sign! God can send *us* to her! We can't miss opportunities to lead single and pregnant mommas back home.

WHAT SEEING HER MIGHT LOOK LIKE

In my first book, I share Jordan's story. Jordan was nineteen years old, pregnant, and unmarried. She joined the Embrace Grace class a little late in the semester, but after we heard her story, we made an exception and allowed her to join us.

Jordan had just found out she was pregnant and was scared. She was an only child, and her mom had left when she was a baby. Their home comprised just Jordan and her father.

When her dad found out about the pregnancy, he was angry and hurt, telling her she was unfit to be a mother and insisting she choose either abortion or adoption. Jordan felt conflicted; in her heart, she wanted to be a mother, but no one in her life agreed. One day, as she tearfully drove herself to work at the UPS shipping store, she cried out to God and asked Him to send someone in whom she could confide, someone who would help her know what to do. In desperation, she said, "God, just send someone today with a package that says the word *church* on it, and then I'll know it's safe for me to ask for help."

The rest of the day crawled by. Lots of customers came to her counter, but none with the package she was looking for. Five minutes prior to the store closing, a man came in with boxes labeled *church*! She knew it must be a sign from God.

She excitedly asked him, "Do you work at a church?" He answered, "No, I have a business that helps churches." As her heart started to sink, the man explained he attended Gateway Church, conveniently located across the street from the store. That was all she needed to hear; this must be her help from God.

Jordan poured out her heart to this stranger, explaining her pregnancy, her loved ones' reactions, and how desperate she was for answers. The father of four listened patiently and reassured her that the church might be able to help. Before he left, the man said some encouraging words and told her he would pray for her. A few days and a few phone calls later, Jordan found herself in our Embrace Grace group, sitting at a table with other single and pregnant young women. As she shared her story, I saw hope in her eyes: finally, someone understood.

What touched me the most is something Jordan said at the end of her story. The subtle beauty of her statement didn't hit me immediately, but it had a time-released impact on my heart: "My dad said I would be a bad mom, but that guy I met at the UPS store said he thought I would be a good mom."

Life-giving words are a rope that can rescue.

That follower of Jesus had spoken words of life into her, right there at the shipping store. He didn't say some profound and beautiful statement that should be hung on a wall somewhere; he just shared from his heart. He may not have thought twice about those words, but to Jordan, they were all she had to hold on to.

Someone believed she could be a good mom, even if that someone was a perfect stranger.

People like Jordan are everywhere. They are working at our grocery stores, bussing our tables, and delivering our packages. We can be searching for the lost everywhere we go. And what then?

Then you are kind.

That's it.

Life-giving words are a rope that can rescue.

There are two kinds of people who stand outside abortion clinics: the ones who yell and scream and the ones who peacefully pray and offer help and hope. The first one makes a woman want to run faster to get inside.

The second one might just make her want to slow down.

Ideas for How to See Her

- Look for wedding rings when encountering pregnant women and engage in an intentional and Holy Spirit-led conversation. Smile and encourage her. See if she will open up and share how she might need support.

- Pass a note of encouragement and hope to a single mom you encounter.

- Lead a 40 Days for Life campaign in your community that aims to end abortion through prayer and fasting, community outreach, and a peaceful all-day vigil in front of abortion businesses.

- If the idea of praying outside an abortion facility intimidates you, try praying from your car and park at an angle so you can see the women walking in. God works through your prayers no matter where you are!

- Find out who leads your local sidewalk counsel group or sidewalk prayer groups and offer to host a meal for the volunteers or provide snacks and water on a hot day when they are serving.

- Ask sidewalk counselors to speak to your church or small group about what they've experienced and how people can get involved.

- If you have artistic gifts, offer to make signs for your local sidewalk groups that are encouraging, uplifting, and full of love.

- Sign up with Sidewalk Advocates for Life for training on how to reach women walking into abortion clinics through a peaceful, prayerful, law-abiding sidewalk advocacy program.

- Connect with a sidewalk counseling ministry and go through their training. Ask a friend to do it with you!

- Create a list of local ministries and resources you can have ready for when you meet a single and pregnant mom—especially your local pro-life pregnancy center, complete with phone numbers. Share that list with friends so you're prepared when God connects you with someone who needs help.

- Reach out to your local high school/college counselors and nurses to make sure they have information about local pregnancy centers or other community resources that can help a new mom who just found out she is pregnant. Also, share your heart and passion with any high school teachers you know and tell them that if they hear or know of any pregnant women in the schools, you would love to connect with them to offer help and support.

- Watch and follow your Facebook Buy/Sell/Trade pages or Marketplace pages for single moms who are asking for gently used baby items or mention needing help. Reach out to see how you can help connect her to people, churches, or ministries in your community.

- Purchase Love Boxes from EmbraceGrace.com and keep one or two in your car, to be available when you might meet someone with an unplanned pregnancy. It's a great tool that inspires a life decision and encourages a young mom who might need hope and community.

- Print an ad in your church directory, bulletin, or website with contact information for the local pregnancy centers and Embrace Grace Support Groups.

- With the permission of the owners of stores that sell baby clothes and supplies, place business cards or flyers that offer help and resources for single moms.

- Connect with your local OB/Gyn offices and place business cards or flyers offering help and resources for single moms.

- Pastors, share from the platform, on occasion, that leaders are here to help if anyone ever experiences an unplanned pregnancy.

- If you are a restaurant owner or have a company with a large number of young workers, try placing help and support flyers in your employee bathrooms with information on where to find help. Provide support hotline phone numbers they can access if they need help or that they can share with a friend who needs help.

- Become a volunteer advocate for your community with Love-Line, an organization that helps single and pregnant moms who feel they have exhausted all opportunities for resources in their area. Through LoveLine, you can search for resources in your area to help women who can't find physical and emotional support in their community.

- Do you love to drive? Become a Stork Bus Volunteer Driver! If you have a flexible schedule, are passionate about ministering in the pro-life movement, and love road trips, connect with Save the Storks or a local pregnancy center near you that has a mobile medical unit. Many pregnancy centers have sonogram machines on vans and busses and will park close to abortion clinics and offer free ultrasounds. The mobile units are beautiful and inviting, with licensed and professional medical staff providing free counsel and medical services.

- On your social media pages, make it known that you are a safe person to talk to if anyone knows someone who needs help because of an unintended pregnancy.

- Marketing and SEO companies, find a pregnancy help organization you love in your community and offer to help with their search engine optimization so women with unplanned pregnancies can find them quickly online. Consider financially supporting pro-life marketing and SEO ministries like Human Coalition and Heroic Media.

- Connect with social workers in your area and provide materials about resources in your community that they can share with women with unplanned pregnancies.

- Organizations with a pro-life focus on outreach for women at abortion centers have all the usual volunteer needs for writers and editors, graphic designers, technology assistance, etc. What might you uniquely offer to support their ministry and keep the ship running?

- Volunteer to make literature packets or "Blessing Bags" for local Sidewalk Advocates. A tutorial is at sidewalkadvocates.org/blessingbags.

National Ministries and Resources

40 Days for Life	40daysforlife.com
Heartbeat International	abortionpillreversal.com
Heroic Media	heroicmedia.org
ICU Mobile	icumobile.org
Human Coalition	humancoalition.org
ProLove Ministries	loveline.com
Save the Storks	savethestorks.com
Sidewalk Advocates for Life	sidewalkadvocates.org

Alliance Defending Freedom created a Legal Guide for Sidewalk Counselors manual to educate you about your legal rights when engaging in sidewalk counseling. Go to adflegal.org for your free download.

Heartbeat's Option Line (800-712-HELP): call or text 24/7 for unplanned pregnancy support.

Prolove Ministries Loveline (888-550-1588): call or text 24/7 for unplanned pregnancy support.

Abortion Pill Rescue (877-558-0333): call or text 24/7 for women who have taken the first dose of the abortion pill (Mifeprex or RU-486) and now regret the decision and wish to reverse the effects.

COMFORT HER

Partnering with Pregnancy Centers

I was speaking at a women's conference out of town, and the host had invited the local Embrace Grace group leaders to a breakfast at her house so they could meet me and another Embrace Grace staff member. One of the group leaders sitting around the table that morning is also a Crisis Counselor at a Life Care Pregnancy Center. Julie was sharing her heart, talking about her work at Life Care, when a sudden question stopped the conversation and silenced the room.

Another leader from another church had brought her mother along to the breakfast. She was visiting from several hours away. Her mother was the one who spoke, through tears, interrupting Julie to ask, "I'm sorry but can I just ask you a quick question? Did your Pregnancy Center used to be called *Life Line Center*?"

Julie answered, "Yes, it was. We opened thirty-three years ago, and that was the original name before we changed it to *Life Care Pregnancy Center*."

The woman started weeping and could barely talk. She explained that, years before, she'd had an unplanned pregnancy and had wanted to carry the baby to term. However, the father of the baby did not agree and began to treat her cruelly. On top of that heartache, her parents expressed their disappointment and disapproval. She began to think terminating the pregnancy was her only option. Heartbroken and alone, she drove to Life Line Center to ask for help and find out where she could get an abortion.

She cried as she shared with Julie that she still remembered the care and compassion she had received. The staff at the center had told her she didn't have to be afraid, they were there to help and support her, whatever she needed. They empowered her and reminded her that she was strong and could do hard things. They gently warned her that an abortion would be something she would probably regret, but she would never regret choosing life.

Because of the love and kindness she experienced at the pregnancy center, this mother *had* chosen life. Now her son is a full-time missionary in Africa, sharing the gospel to change the world.

WHAT THE BIBLE HAS TO SAY
ABOUT PARTNERING WITH OTHERS TO RESCUE

If someone were drowning in the ocean, we would call the Coast Guard and pray for the first responders to arrive on the scene quickly. They have the expertise to go into places the average person cannot. They enter immediate danger to save. That is their only goal.

A first responder doesn't pull the rescued soul to safety only to chastise them for wading too far out into the ocean. Neither do they give the rescued person an in-depth lesson about how he or she could have avoided drowning in the first place.

Pregnancy centers are the first responders for women with unplanned pregnancies. Women often feel as if they are drowning when they learn they are pregnant. They can't catch their breath. They feel like they are slipping away from the world they once knew.

Pregnancy centers are a place of refuge and help in a woman's time of need. The responsibility to save women should not fall solely on their shoulders, but as first responders, they have been called to the ministry of comfort.

Paul explains where comfort comes from in 2 Corinthians 1:3–5: "Praise be to the God and Father of our Lord Jesus Christ, the Father of compassion and the God of all comfort, who comforts us in all our troubles, so that we can comfort those in any trouble with the comfort we ourselves receive from God. For just as we share abundantly in the sufferings of Christ, so also our comfort abounds through Christ."

The Holy Spirit is our Comforter. Jesus knew we would need the Comforter because life would be uncomfortable sometimes. And when we are outside our comfort zones, we experience the supernatural comfort of our heavenly Father. Are we willing to stand up, get uncomfortable, and step out with bold courage?

One person who left his comfort zone was Peter. Matthew 14:22–33 describes how the disciples leave the crowds ahead of Jesus in a boat. During the night, Jesus appears to them on the water, making the disciples freak out! But Peter takes a deep breath, gathers his courage, and asks Jesus to prove He is who He says He is.

> "Lord, if it's you," Peter replied, "tell me to come to you on the water."
>
> "Come," he said.
>
> Then Peter got down out of the boat, walked on the water and came toward Jesus. But when he saw the wind, he was afraid and, beginning to sink, cried out, "Lord, save me!"
>
> Immediately Jesus reached out his hand and caught him. "You of little faith," he said, "why did you doubt?"
>
> And when they climbed into the boat, the wind died down.

Jesus doesn't call us out of the boat just to see us struggle and drown in our problems. He doesn't just say "Good luck" and let us figure things out on our own. He goes with us to those places of unfamiliarity and helps us be brave. We have to keep our eyes fixed on Him with unshakable faith. Peter believed he could do something radical with Jesus—and it began by having enough faith to step out.

Knowing God is always with us can lead us beyond a life of apathy to a life of tenacious bravery and open-handed grace.

Finding your place to serve in

the pro-life movement will take some courage, and it might feel uncomfortable, but you will have front-row seats to see God at work. And you will never take a step alone. Jesus promised, "And surely I am with you always, to the very end of the age" (Matt. 28:20). Just knowing God is always with us can lead us beyond a life of apathy to a life of tenacious bravery and open-handed grace.

When we ask a single mother to carry her baby to term, we are asking her to have enough courage to take a step out of her comfort zone.

And we can't ask her to step out when *we* aren't willing to do it too.

DISCOVERING YOUR PLACE

Pregnancy centers are local, non-profit organizations that provide compassionate support to women and men faced with difficult pregnancy decisions. They are usually faith-based and are made possible by people like you and me. There are thousands of pregnancy centers all over the United States that offer free services like pregnancy testing, information about options, resources for help in their communities, and post-decision support like parenting education and abortion recovery groups. Many give out free diapers and wipes or have boutiques with gently used baby items for mommas in need. Some pregnancy centers even offer consultations with licensed medical professionals and STD testing.

Pregnancy centers also offer ultrasounds for pregnancy confirmation. Sonogram machines have become great tools to help save lives. The National Institute of Family and Life Advocates

(NIFLA), a national legal network of pro-life pregnancy centers, say that about 78 percent of mothers who saw an ultrasound image of their unborn child before deciding about abortion ended up choosing life.[1] There is nothing more emotionally engaging than the sight of the baby kicking and moving on the screen or hearing their little heartbeat. My friends who are so-nogram technicians say they have watched the initial panic in a young woman's eyes melt into tenderness and protectiveness when they see their baby for the first time through an ultrasound. Focus on the Family provides grants for ultrasound machines and nurses' training for pregnancy centers through their Option Ultrasound program. Since 2004, their program has helped save more than 459,000 lives![2] All of this and more is offered at minimal cost to the pregnancy centers.

Perhaps the most amazing thing about pregnancy centers is that many are staffed by volunteers and funded by donors through local churches.

Pregnancy centers can be considered first responders because they know all the resources available in their communities and can help a woman make a more informed decision about her pregnancy. I've seen pregnancy centers give information about programs for childcare subsidy, health care support, housing and maternity homes, as well as job information, to name just a few. When a new mom knows she is not alone, she feels a renewed peace of mind. She might not have everything figured out, but she can relax, knowing there are people and programs that will help.

Best of all, pregnancy centers are a great referral source to help connect moms to a local church. Often volunteers and staff share the gospel with a visiting mom, and they pray she will get connected to a church family. But most women experiencing an unplanned pregnancy are hesitant to go to church. They have come to expect rejection.

Embrace Grace uses Love Boxes to help mommas feel love from a local church before they ever step foot into the building. Each box is packed like a special gift, with tissue and a bright bow. All Love Boxes include an invitation to the church, along with a onesie that has *Best Gift Ever* printed on the front. There is also a *Brave* Journal, *A Bump in Life* book, and a hand-written letter of encouragement, written by our volunteers.

We distribute Love Boxes to pregnancy centers within thirty miles of a church with an Embrace Grace support group. The pregnancy center gives the Love Boxes to women who have just found out they are pregnant. Our hope is that the gift inspires her to choose life, makes her feel loved, and helps her get connected to an Embrace Grace group for continued support (for how-to, look for "Love Box" at embracegrace.com).

WHAT COMFORTING HER MIGHT LOOK LIKE

Don't miss the opportunity to host a Love Box packing party as a fun outreach event at your church! Organize your members to fold the onesies, write the encouragement letters, package everything beautifully, and pray over each box. Then you can deliver the boxes to pregnancy centers in your area. Love Boxes have proven to be a powerful and almost irresistible invitation for moms to come to the Embrace Grace support group at the church providing them.

Another way to help is to volunteer directly at a pregnancy center. They are always in need of helping hands.

If you are a nurse or sonographer, a pregnancy center is a great way to serve by using your unique skillset. Once a week or several times a week, you can volunteer your time by providing medical counsel and ultrasound services to women facing one of the most important decisions of their lives.

Pregnancy centers are always in need of helping hands.

If you have a knack for administration, volunteering at the front desk or setting up the baby boutique is a delightful way to serve.

If you enjoy social interaction and love to encourage, you can volunteer as a client advocate who provides a listening ear to moms, or you might teach a parenting class.

There are important jobs for introverts, too. From the comfort of your own home and on your own schedule, you can write the *Dear Brave Girl* letters that are included in Love Boxes.

There are many other ways to serve. No matter what your gifts may be, pregnancy centers can use your help!

Recently, I had the pleasure of meeting Tansy, a new momma who tells her own story about the influence of a pregnancy center in her life:

> I'm just emerging from such a dark season of life. At the end of 2017, my husband, Todd, fell into a deep depression, and his addiction gained full control of his soul. We made poor choices together, and I tried methamphetamine with him. We lost our home, vehicles,

and belongings. Our marriage wasn't even hanging on by a single thread. Todd's addiction took over, and he became very abusive.

At the end of February 2018, I sought refuge with some friends that he introduced me to, and I left my home, my whole life, everything he and I worked hard to accomplish together. I asked my in-laws to care for our children because I needed to figure out *how* to fend for myself. In March of 2018 Todd put his hands around my neck, and the neighbors witnessed what happened. In April of 2018 while visiting with our two beautiful children under the supervision of my sister-in-law, we found out Todd had died of an overdose. We don't know who he was with or who dropped his lifeless body off at the emergency room, but the addiction won.

I became hyper-focused, seeking a place to make a new home for the kids and me. I got an apartment in June of 2018 and then faced a rough custody battle with my in-laws over my children. I was so angry and scared. I remember lying on the floor of the three-bedroom apartment I worked so hard to get and just wanting to peacefully leave this earth. A few days later, I finally got up and went to Wal-Mart. I had a feeling I needed to take a pregnancy test. After I peed on the stick, it immediately showed up pregnant. I was in *shock*. I felt like it had to be wrong. It just couldn't be. So I took *seven* more tests. They were all positive.

I felt so much shame. I was embarrassed by my actions. How could I have been so careless? This pregnancy was not from my husband, who had died two months prior. I contacted the father, and we both decided termination was the most logical thing to do. I made an appointment with a pregnancy center to learn about my options. I went alone and spoke with a sweet advocate who presented me an array of information on abortion, adoption, and parenting. She was so encouraging and made me feel so much better. She handed me a pretty white box with a big pink tulle bow that said, "Love in a Box." I left my appointment, went to my car, and opened that box in the parking lot. Inside was an invitation to join a group called Embrace Grace—a support group for young women experiencing unintended pregnancies. There was a handwritten note of encouragement and a tiny baby onesie that said, "Best Gift Ever." That's the moment when life chose me.

Ellie was born in March, 2019, and my other two children finally came home just a few months later. All my babies were together.

Through it all, I have renewed my relationship with God, and He's using my story to help bring all of His children home. Just as hard as I worked to prove I was fit to be a mother for all of my children, God was showing me that I'm *His* daughter. And my Ellie is a blessing from God! She's the baby we didn't know we needed! I will never forget the love and support I received at the pregnancy center and through Embrace Grace. I go to my new church twice per week, once to be filled up on Sunday morning and once to lead Embrace Grace. I get to pour into women who are hurting and scared just like women poured into me when I needed it most. My life has changed forever.

We want more women like Tansy to have a life-changing encounter with a kindhearted person at a pregnancy center. But it will take more volunteers to meet the increasing demand. There is an urgent need for support and involvement in your local pregnancy centers, and they would love to partner with you to meet women's needs through pregnancy and beyond. Please reach out to schedule a tour and ask them how you can serve. One email or phone call is all it takes.

Then you will be a first responder, too.

Ideas for How to Comfort Her

- Contact your local pregnancy center, schedule a tour, and ask what their greatest needs are and how you can help.

- Be a client advocate who meets with clients before medical staff to listen, comfort, educate, and support.

- Do you have special training or skillset that a single and pregnant mom might benefit from learning? Teach a class at a pregnancy center on topics like parenting, life skills, childbirth, or financial management. Got another topic to teach? Just ask your local pregnancy center to see if they think the moms might benefit from your knowledge.

- Mentor a single and pregnant mom throughout her pregnancy through your local center.

- Are you administratively gifted? Volunteer at the front desk and answer calls for the pregnancy center.

- Calling all licensed nurses and sonographers! You can serve shifts at a pregnancy center and help save lives!

- We can't forget the men who need support. If you are a guy who would love to mentor new dads, sign up through your local pregnancy center to see how you can help.

- Throw a baby shower for one or several of the pregnancy center clients. Set up Amazon wish lists and partner with local churches.

- Volunteer with the baby boutique at your center by going through gently used donations, setting up the boutique, and keeping it stocked.

- Launder gently used baby clothes that are donated to the center. Clean and disinfect donated baby items.

- Are you a hostess with the mostest? Serve by planning and producing fundraising events for the pregnancy center.

- Calling all decorators and people with great taste, who could help spruce up the center or redecorate the lobby or client areas. Use your skills to decorate for their next fundraising gala!

- Stuff, lick, and stamp a pregnancy center's mass mailings who go out with updates and ways to partner.

- Be a church ambassador for your local pregnancy center by spreading the word about events and opportunities to serve.

- Be a student ambassador at your school and represent your local pregnancy center to let students know there is support and help if a student experiences an unplanned pregnancy. Become known as a safe person to talk to.

- Be an influencer for your local center! Share their social media graphics and post about ways to get involved.

- Serve your center by cleaning and tidying up weekly or monthly.

- Serve your center by doing yard work or building maintenance.

- Bundle diapers and wipes for quick access for single moms who have a need.

- Serve on the board of directors for your center.

- For your next birthday, have your friends donate baby items instead of birthday gifts, so you can give them to your local center.

- Set an alarm to remind yourself to pray for your local pregnancy center every day.

- Offer to bring lunch, sweets, or frappuccinos for your local pregnancy center staff.

- Host a Share the Love Outreach event at your church. Gather church members together to assemble Embrace Grace Love Boxes and then give them to your local pregnancy center to place in the hands of women with unplanned pregnancies.

- Mail cards of encouragement to your pregnancy center staff.

- Give monthly to the closest pregnancy center in your area.

- Invite a pregnancy center leader to share their mission with your church or business.

- Be a prayer warrior at your center. Volunteer to pray for each woman who walks through the door.

- Practice drive-by prayers! Every time you pass your local pregnancy center, pray for the staff, volunteers, and clients.

- Partner with your pregnancy center by hosting a baby bottle drive. They provide you with baby bottles for your church, neighbors, and business friends to fill with spare change, cash, and checks. Gather the bottles at the end of the drive, and deliver them to your local center.

- Host a diaper drive with your friends or your church. Donate the diapers to the local pregnancy center. They have a continuous need for diapers and wipes.

- Support Focus on the Family's Ultrasound Grant program to help get ultrasound technology into more pregnancy centers, a valuable tool that helps save lives.

Find a Pregnancy Center through National Resources

Use a search engine, typing in your city's name and the words *pregnancy center*, or connect with one of these national sources of information:

Care Net	care-net.org
Focus on the Family	focusonthefamily.com/pro-life
Heartbeat International	heartbeatinternational.org
Pregnancy Decision Line	pregnancydecisionline.org
Option Line	optionline.org

3

WELCOME HER

Opening the Doors to Community

A few years ago, a pastor called our Embrace Grace offices to find out what Embrace Grace was all about. Something unusual had happened at a local coffee shop. The pastor was talking with another pastor when a young woman walked up to their table and nervously handed him a folded piece of paper. Then she immediately turned and left the building. He was surprised by what it said and called me to find out more about Embrace Grace. I was intrigued and asked him to scan it and send me a copy. Here's what the young woman gave this pastor:

Hi I'm very shy and I don't mean to bother you. I didn't intend to listen but I couldn't help but over hear. Please keep doing your work for the broken, it must be hard and so much easier to focus on normal church people - but its us that need you the most. The most broken people only run from the church because we feel unaccepted, we feel how much work we are, we feel like burdens. We also feel like most people in the church want nothing to do with us because we may not live ideally. We may be strippers just trying to feed our kids and get through nursing school to give them a better life. We may be hurting for the whole world, and sometimes the "TV" and "political" christians aren't what we think Jesus really wanted. We may have grown up in church but felt pushed out when we had big questions - because they required perhaps uncomfortable answers and discussions. Please keep listening to the broken, they need you more than anyone. they need the church when they are on drugs. They need the church if they are gay. They need the church if they are homeless. They need the church if they are prostitutes. They need the church if they are teen mothers. They need you. I'm sorry if this is weird. I have horrible anxiety so I can't approach people with words, I can only write.

Also, this women does crazy good stuff for Jesus and has brought so many young ladies to God through love. Her name is Amy Ford — Embracegrace.com She's always looking for more churches to get involved.

Keep up the love, always always use love; because the broken have had enough hate

— Just a broken mom trying to put it all together

WHAT THE BIBLE HAS TO SAY
ABOUT OPENING THE DOORS

Last year a woman approached me at a pregnancy center conference. She had heard me speak a few hours earlier. She seemed very concerned and shared how she was struggling with some of the things she had heard me say. She said, "I see young women at my church who strive to stay pure and abstain from sex before marriage. It's so hard, but they are doing so well at putting God first in every area. But then there are the girls who have sex before marriage and get pregnant. And you're saying the church should throw them a baby shower and honor them for choosing life. Isn't that saying it's okay to do what they did? Isn't that condoning sin? How is that fair?"

That's when I heard a whisper in my spirit about the story of the prodigal son. In Luke 15:11–32, Jesus tells an unforgettable story. A father has two sons, and the younger son asks for his share of the inheritance early. The father divides the property between the brothers and watches the young one leave home.

The younger son takes the money and sets off toward a distant country, where he wastes it on sinful escapades. Before long, he loses his share of the inheritance and ends up working in a pig pen, hungry and alone.

Filled with shame, guilt, and remorse, the son heads home with his head hanging low. By that time, he is willing to endure his father's punishment or scorn. He is sure even the worst scenario would be better than the lousy life he has been living. With every unpaved, rough, and rocky step he takes, he thinks of what his father might say to him and wonders if he will be rejected.

He thinks about the mess he's gotten himself into and hammers himself with regret.

If you've heard this story before, then you know that punishment is not on the agenda that day.

A *party* is.

Verse 20 says, "But while he was still a long way off, his father saw him and was filled with compassion for him; he ran to his son, threw his arms around him and kissed him."

The father had been waiting for him and recognizes his son even from a long distance. He doesn't hesitate but runs to his son with outstretched arms. He doesn't greet his son with reminders of all the things he has done wrong; he doesn't discipline or chastise him. The father gives his wayward son a giant hug and kisses him. He is so glad to see his son has finally come home. The son feels undeserving of his father's love, but it does not deter the father from lavishing love upon him.

Then the son's jaw drops as the servants of his father's household throw him a celebration fit for royalty. He had never expected a warm homecoming like this. Even after all he has squandered and wasted, the father is delighted to see him again. He wants everyone to celebrate!

But one person isn't in the mood.

The older brother is in the field working. When he comes closer to the house, he hears a big party taking place and asks the servants about all the commotion. As soon as he learns what it is, he becomes so angry, he does not even attend the banquet to see his brother. He cannot understand how his father could be celebrating after all his younger brother has done. Blinded by a bitter heart and the inability to forgive, he doesn't see beyond his brother's irresponsibility to the redemption and healing happening right in front of him.

Leading in Embrace Grace, I see beautiful daughters who are walking that tiresome, difficult, jagged, and unpaved road back home. They certainly don't think they are worthy to be a daughter of the heavenly Father, but they are drawn by the idea that maybe—just maybe—if they work hard enough, they might be a servant. With the noise of shame and regret drowning out all hope, they assume church will only highlight their sins and past choices.

But miraculous healing occurs when they do not receive the rejection they expect. Many women do not know that God never cruelly yells at His children. He never talks down to them or rubs their noses in their wrongdoing. It tends to surprise an unmarried mother when she is welcomed into the family of God. If the church opens the doors to community, she learns about a Father who runs to her, even when she is still "a long way off." She learns about a heavenly Father who wraps his arms around her, kisses her, and draws her near.

As a young woman processes this God who expresses unconditional love for her, she is blown away to be invited to a celebration in her own honor. Max Lucado offers an excellent picture of grace in one of my favorite quotes: "The difference between mercy and grace? Mercy gave the Prodigal Son a second chance. Grace gave him a feast."[1]

It makes me consider which is the greater honor, that God throws a celebration for each of us when we return to Him or that

He entrusts us with the privilege of throwing a celebration *for* others when they return to Him.

What a pity that the older brother missed the precious opportunity to partner with his father. The father didn't throw a party for him, but it could be that the father felt he could bless his oldest son *even more* by inviting him to help host a celebration for someone else.

Through Embrace Grace, the church has an opportunity to throw a single and pregnant mom a few parties, like the baby showers and Princess Day. Baby showers are thrown by churches all over the nation, celebrating the lives of babies who will be born and change the world someday. People come with gifts specially chosen in the moms' favorite colors and patterns for her baby. It's a beautiful celebration of life. At my church, the baby showers are my favorite events! We honor thirty to forty moms at one big party twice a year. Hundreds of church members attend, and each table designated for a mom is stacked so high with gifts that the moms can barely see the stage! At the end, a pastor speaks, shares the prodigal son story, and makes an altar call. Time after time, we have seen women give their lives to the Lord at these baby showers. It is more than just a party here on earth. It is a party in heaven!

Princess Day is another event in the Embrace Grace curriculum that celebrates each single and pregnant mom and the end of the Embrace Grace experience. A make-up and hair team from the church come and volunteer their time to help make the mommas feel beautiful on the outside. Then the Embrace Grace leaders crown each mom and speak a blessing over her, reminding her that she is a daughter of the Most High and beautiful on the inside. They remind her that God has made her strong. They tell her she is a Princess Warrior, equipped by the King of Kings for any battle in her future. They remind her that she is a fierce woman in God's Kingdom, propelled by the wind of His Spirit. The celebration ends with a beautiful dinner. It is a memory we hope will be sealed in their hearts forever.

Christianity isn't just about accepting Jesus into our hearts and then coasting through life until we die. No, salvation is just the beginning. It's the invitation to live a kingdom life in which we love with words but also with actions and truth. We can play a significant role in His plan of redemption by celebrating all who return, knowing they are back where they belong.

DISCOVERING YOUR PLACE

How many times have we forfeited the opportunity to celebrate our brothers and sisters, even while they are "a long way off"? We are invited to partner with God in welcoming others home not because of how "good" we have been, but because celebration is in our DNA. We are His children, and this is what His family does. Our whole life is a dance; we are designed to celebrate God and celebrate others with love. We get to partner with heaven and receive and give grace, loving extravagantly.

Not everyone is ready to do that. Just a few weeks ago the Embrace Grace staff received a message from a pastor who has completed one semester of the Embrace Grace curriculum. He explained that he would like to move forward with the next semester of new moms but only if we agreed to a few adjustments.

His stipulations were that we would "never use the word *decorations* or *party* and never wrap any presents." He didn't want his church community to know what they were doing for the young mothers: "to give the wrong message in any way that we are celebrating a baby born out of wedlock." He wanted never to "say babies are 'a blessing from God'" or to "tell a lost girl she is a princess."

> **God's love is a magnet that pulls hearts toward Him.**

He wanted to keep the baby showers and Princess Day activities off the church's emailed and online publications, suggesting that these changes would protect his church community from "heartbreak."

But the changes he suggested would only perpetuate the shame culture in the church. No wonder the abortion rate is the same inside the church as it is outside the church. Practices like these do not improve the statistics.

Needless to say, the Embrace Grace program declined the opportunity to partner with this church. When a woman who has an unplanned pregnancy is brave enough to try church for the first time, we hope it can feel like a homecoming and not a prison sentence. Shame doesn't make someone want to do the right thing. It makes people want to run away, hide, and isolate.

But God's love doesn't work that way. It is a magnet that pulls hearts toward Him.

No one can conceive life without the consent of God, the author of life. The baby is not a sin. A baby is a miracle. All lives, no matter how they got here, should be celebrated. Through the simple act of throwing a party, prodigals might finally feel like they have come home.

Once an Embrace Grace momma was so overwhelmed with the number of baby shower gifts that were just for her, she stood about ten feet away, temporarily paralyzed by the church's generosity. She had missed quite a few of the classes, and the leaders were having a hard time connecting with her. But in that moment, everything changed. She had her hands over her mouth, with tears streaming down her cheeks.

She kept saying over and over, "I don't deserve this. I don't deserve this."

The truth is, none of us do.

WHAT WELCOMING HER CAN LOOK LIKE

Rachel came to every session of the twelve-week Embrace Grace support group at her church. She was heavy-hearted because her mom was upset with her for getting pregnant. Their once-close relationship had been fractured, and she went home every day feeling more and more shame. She and her mother fought a lot because her mom was sorely disappointed, wanting a better life for her daughter.

When the church threw the baby shower for all the young women in Embrace Grace, Rachel didn't think her mother would come. Hundreds of church members gathered to shower the single moms with gifts that day. Just as Rachel sat down to open her gifts, she looked up and saw her mom walk into the room. Her mother nervously sat next to her. She watched Rachel open her gifts, one by one—gifts given by strangers who were smiling and celebrating her brave decision to choose life. Rachel's mother's heart began to soften. She reached her hand over and placed it on Rachel's pregnant belly and held it there as tears streamed down her face. Rachel placed her hand over her mother's, and they wept together. Love heals hearts and binds us together.

That night, Rachel's mom said, "Thank you all for the baby shower today. I am still having a hard time accepting the reality that things just didn't turn out the way I planned for my daughter. But I know that our God has greater plans for my daughter. I know that everything goes through His hands first and that my daughter and her fiancé will be a walking testimony one day. All glory to God! My coming to the shower was a last-minute decision, and I am ever so grateful for the tugging of the Lord and His prompting me to go and support my girl. As I walked in, I was so overwhelmed by 1) the presence of the Holy Spirit and 2) the generosity of His children. I have not fully supported my daughter through most of this pregnancy because I was still dealing and healing (and still am doing so), but today I couldn't be more thankful for the ministry of Embrace Grace. You have truly helped and supported her when I didn't or couldn't. So thank you. I am truly able to begin the healing process and be there more for her now. Today the Lord also reminded me of my dreams . . . He has begun to chisel at this hardened heart so His will can be done and completed in my life as well as in my daughter's."

As the church accepts the invitation to celebrate God's sons and daughters, we see transformation happen.

As the church accepts the invitation to celebrate God's sons and daughters, we see transformation happen in front of our very eyes.

One semester we had a beautiful, young, and pregnant momma who had heard about Embrace Grace from a friend. She did not have transportation so I agreed to pick her up and take her home every week so she could come to the class. The day I met her, she hopped in my car and seemed nervous. She said her name was Brooke, and as we drove to the first class she asked a lot of questions. Before we got too far into conversation, she stopped me and said, "I'm a wiccan. I believe in witchcraft. I'm mainly coming because my friend invited me and for the free stuff. Is that going to be a problem?"

I smiled and said, "Of course not. You are welcome at church. I'm so happy that you want to come!"

Over the course of the semester we had extra time together outside of the class because of our carpool time, as well as a few coffee dates. We sometimes talked about casual things, like details about her day or about her dog. As our friendship grew, she started opening up about her hopes and dreams for her baby and how she wished things had worked out with the father of the baby. Eventually our conversations veered into theology. This nineteen-year-old had done her research about religions, but she stood her ground on what she believed. She never missed one class.

I once overheard her say, "I like the way it makes me feel when I come here." That stuck with me. She liked the way it made her feel, even though she didn't believe anything we were saying when we spoke about a heavenly Father who loved her. She may not have realized it at the time, but what she was feeling was the presence and love of God when she walked in the doors every week.

The semester was drawing to a close. She attended the big baby shower and enjoyed our Princess Day finale. After our last class, I dropped her at home. As we said goodbye, it didn't sound as if she ever planned to go to church again.

My heart sank as I drove away. Tears stung my cheeks as I thought about how I had invested so much time in her, and we connected so well. It didn't end the way I had hoped it would. As I drove, I cried out to God, "Why didn't she choose You when surely she knows now that You chose her? She loved the class. She never missed a week! God, why? Did we do something wrong? Am I missing something?"

I took it personally.

Pulling into my driveway that night, I felt the Lord say, "You planted seeds. You created a safe place for her to attend church when she might never have tried it otherwise. Now leave the rest to Me."

I took a deep breath and accepted the situation for what it was and how it had ended. Over the next few months, I would check in on Brooke from time to time to see how she was doing. She always seemed fine and desired to keep the conversation light.

About a year after going through the Embrace Grace program, Brooke called me out of the blue, so excited she could barely speak. She said, "Amy, you will never believe what happened! I don't know why, but the past few months I kept thinking about Embrace Grace and God. I would think that maybe He really is real and maybe He is trying to talk to me. I would get feelings and little signs that He was hearing what I was thinking—things no one knew. As I pulled up to work today, I said out loud in my car, 'God if you're real, can you give me a sign? Like, something so obvious I can't ever question whether you are real or not. I'll just know it.' Then I went into work at the gas station, and this random man walked up to my counter kind of nervous-like and said, 'God wants you to know that the light is there. Whatever you are struggling with is almost over, and you can do this. Be patient and you can make it through. Just accept Him into your life and believe in Him.' Can you believe it? God is real! I went straight home and got my curriculum from Embrace Grace and found the salvation prayer, and I prayed it! I put the tiara on my head and looked in the mirror when I prayed because I wanted it to be a moment I would never forget. I believe in God and know that He died for me and that He really loves me! I surrendered my life to Him, and I am His daughter!"

With tears streaming down my face, I looked up to heaven and whispered, "Thank You!"

I caught a few glimpses of our sweet Brooke after that day when her life changed. I would occasionally see her at church, with her tattoos, piercings, and gauges, her arms outstretched to heaven during worship, her husband and daughter singing right by her side. Small seeds of love have bloomed into a beautiful garden, and it all started because she liked the welcome she felt when she came to church.

The church can change lives just by making people feel important. When we love people and are obedient to plant seeds, we can trust God to coordinate the watering and growth. He loves to woo His daughters' hearts to His. Sometimes He will use a church to do it. Sometimes He will use strangers.

And sometimes He will use a baby.

Ideas for How to Welcome Her

- Foster a culture of vulnerability and authenticity within your church. Share your struggles and your stories. Be real with each other. This helps a newcomer know that church is a safe place when she needs help. Pastor, that goes for you too. Culture starts from the top and works its way down.

- Start an Embrace Grace group at your church to disciple and mentor single and pregnant women.

- Start an Embrace Life support group at your church to disciple and mentor single young moms.

- Throw a baby shower for single and pregnant moms at your church. Assemble a team of volunteers who are excited to serve.

- Connect with your local pregnancy center and let them know their clients are welcome at your church.

- Speak about abortion from the pulpit on occasion (more often than just Sanctity of Life Sunday) and share that there is hope and healing with Jesus.

- Start an abortion healing group at your church. If you don't feel called to lead it, ask God to show you someone that might want to. You can be the activator!

- Discuss abortion healing and support systems for single and pregnant moms frequently at your church so your members know that if they or their loved ones find themselves in that situation, the church is a safe place for them.

- Go out into your communities and find single and pregnant moms and invite them in. They are everywhere. Encourage other members of the church to do the same. (See chapter 1 on ways to find her.)

- Teach a pro-love and pro-life message on Sanctity of Life Sunday (always in January). Any pro-life message must be approached with biblical truth and sensitivity toward people in your congregation who might have experienced abortion. Invite other pro-life ministries in your community to share and set up tables with information about how to get involved.

- Make this book available to your congregation and challenge them to undertake each year one to five of the recommended action steps.

- Start a single parent ministry at your church.

- Offer or teach a Christian Pro-Life Apologetics class and walk through what the Bible says about the issue of life.

- Highlight local pro-life organizations and your local pregnancy centers throughout the year at the church.

- Review your church's policy with leadership, making sure that all ministry staff and personnel know they should never refer a member for an abortion and that your church will not tolerate abuse of power or bullying, but with high ethics and motivation you will protect the vulnerable. Many moms with unplanned pregnancies have church wounds or a distorted

HELP HER BE BRAVE

view of what the church is for. Careful policies can help create a safe place, where a pregnant woman can come to for help.

- Compile pro-life resources and share it with your church leaders. Ask how you can champion the pro-life cause and be a point person for help within the church if someone finds themselves with an unplanned pregnancy.

- Develop an emergency stockpile of gently-used baby and children items at your church for single moms or foster families in need.

- Challenge family members within your church to adopt or foster children in your community.

- Host a single-parent ministry night! Offer childcare and give parents the opportunity to be poured into, loved on, and supported. If the budget allows, have dinner as a group once a month.

- Start a *Making Life Disciples* program at your church. This program trains your church to approach unplanned pregnancies with the same discipleship lens your church uses to address issues of hunger, grief, poverty, and addiction.

- Partner with local maternity homes for homeless single and pregnant women. Financially support the great work they are doing. Maybe encouraging a ministry team or small group to volunteer to clean for a day or redecorate one of their bedrooms. Bring them lunch one day and share what God has been teaching and showing you. Ask the House Parents about their greatest needs, and rally your church to meet the needs.

- Find a local abortion healing support group (if there is not one at your church), so you can refer a friend who has opened up to you about her need. Connect with Support After Abortion to find a group near you.

- Take up an offering for pro-life ministries. Build into your outreach budget to support local pregnancy centers.

- Host a diaper drive at your church and donate to your local center or food pantry.

- Host a Back-to-School event for single parents. Have them meet at a store so your ministry budget can cover the school supplies for their kids up to a certain amount. That way the mom can pick out her kids' favorite brands and colors.

- Plan a "Life Night" for your youth group to educate teens about a biblical pro-life position and how that's lived out.

- Host a movie night to show a movie like *Unplanned* and then discuss with attendees what it means to be pro-life.

- Have your church bless single moms at Christmas time by providing them gift cards. Host a Christmas event for single moms where they can pick up their gift card and leave their kids for a few hours at the church for a fun night while mom gets to go shopping for the family kid-free!

- Look for and support pro-life efforts already happening at your church. Talk with your members, asking around for those who are involved in ministries like foster care, pregnancy support, or abortion healing. Chances are, there may be super-passionate people you can link arms with and make an even greater impact.

- To learn more, attend a pro-life conference like March for Life or the Pro-Life Women's Conference. Consider attending an adoption and foster care conference like Christian Alliance for Orphans.

- Have the Pro-Grace team come to your church and host a training workshop on what grace looks like for the woman with an unplanned pregnancy. You will learn how to take the politics out of the discussion and allow love to heal her. You will be empowered and equipped to release grace in the discussion of abortion.

- Find an international pro-life cause you or your church can support and pray for.

- Ask your pastor how you can help the church champion life in your community. Come to the meeting with ideas!

- Host a pastors' luncheon and invite local pastors to come and hear about ways their church can engage in the community to help save lives.

- Ask your pastor if you can sponsor snacks for their next staff meeting and for ten minutes to share about resources in your community so the ministry team knows how to help connect women who are abortion-vulnerable to ministry resources.

- Highlight Orphan Sunday at your church (in November) and inspire your congregation to support foster families or become a foster family. Christian Alliance for Orphans has great tools and ideas.

- Play videos for your congregations highlighting pro-life testimonials or the great work pro-life organizations are doing in your communities.

- Begin training on how to become a foster family or host training events for foster families that inspire and equip. Check out LifeLine for great resources.

- Host a Share the Love Outreach, gathering your church members to assemble Embrace Grace Love Boxes. Give the boxes to your local pregnancy center to place in the hands of women with unplanned pregnancies.

National Organizations to Serve and Support

Christian Alliance for Orphans	cafo.org
Embrace Grace	embracegrace.com
LifeLine Children's Services	lifelinechild.org
Making Life Disciples	makinglifedisciples.com
March for Life	marchforlife.org
Pro-Grace	prograce.org
Pro-Life Women's Conference	prolifewomen.com
Support After Abortion	supportafterabortion.com

4

PROTECT HER

Speaking Up for the Powerless

My phone rang one afternoon, and it was a mom named Miranda who had been through Embrace Grace a few years earlier. She was upset because she had a feeling that her sister, Madi, might be pregnant and have scheduled an abortion. She told me, "Madi asked me if I would pick her up from work and drive her to a doctor's appointment and then drive her home afterward. She has a procedure scheduled. When I asked her what it was for, she wouldn't tell me. That's not like her. She has been acting *off* lately. I have a feeling she's going to get an abortion. What do I do? I don't want her to be upset or pull away from me if I press her about it."

We encouraged Miranda to be brave and to approach Madi about it later that night after work. We dropped a Love Box on her doorstep to help guide the conversation. With a gift in her hand and love in her heart, we believed Madi might listen to Miranda's plea to choose life.

Then we prayed all night for Miranda's courage to have the conversation and Madi's courage to cancel the appointment.

Miranda called me the next morning and said, "We talked. She was a little upset with me, but she took the box. She didn't want to discuss it much. The abortion is still scheduled for later today. I'm picking her up from work to take her. She's already paid for it. Please be praying."

We went straight to social media to ask everyone to pray for a mom who had an abortion scheduled later that same day, praying that she would be brave, choose life, and have peace in her heart and mind. Within minutes, we were flooded with comments of people saying they were praying. People shared the post again and again. It had hundreds of views and interactions. We had an army of prayer warriors, all praying for this sweet baby and amazing mom.

Later that day, Miranda called to give me an update. I was breathless as I listened. She had picked up Madi from work at the scheduled time, but when she got in the car, Madi had broken down and cried. She just couldn't go through with the abortion.

We put the good news on social media, and thousands celebrated another life saved. Madi went on to go through Embrace Grace and had the cutest little boy. She's a great mom, and the best part? Now she works for us at Embrace Grace headquarters.

Her sister was an advocate for Madi and her son, as she boldly approached her with a Love Box in hand, asking her to reconsider her abortion decision.

WHAT THE BIBLE HAS TO SAY
ABOUT SPEAKING UP FOR THE POWERLESS

Over and over in Scripture, God uses people who show courage, people who stand up when everyone else sits down. One of my favorite examples of that kind of strength is Esther. You can read the book of Esther in the Bible to be inspired by her powerful story.

This classic story of murder and suspense involves four main characters. The first is our heroine, Esther, a Jewish girl who has been taken captive. The second is Mordecai, Esther's cousin, who has raised her after her parents died. The third is King Xerxes, who needs a new queen and selects Esther from many young women. And the fourth and final player in this drama is the villain, Haman, a high-ranking advisor to the king.

Haman does not like the Jews, so he manipulates King Xerxes into making a decree that all Jews should be destroyed. The king has no idea that his newly chosen queen, Esther, is Jewish.

Esther knows she must act fast, becoming an advocate for her beloved people, or they will meet their doom. As time continues to tick away, she knows she must plead with the king to spare the lives of the Jews.

But she faces a life-threatening problem: According to the custom of the time, she could be killed for approaching the king in boldness, asking him to rethink his edict. Anyone who enters the throne room without being invited could be sentenced to death. By approaching her husband when he has not asked to see her, Esther could lose her life.

But she also could lose her life if the edict proceeds according to Haman's evil plan.

There is only one thing to do. Esther, her servants, Mordecai, and all the Jewish people pray. Esther decides there is no turning back. She determines to be obedient and brave, going before the king no matter the results.

With extraordinary courage, Esther stands up for her people when no one else will, even at the risk of losing her life: "On the third day Esther put on her royal robes and stood in the inner court of the palace, in front of the king's hall. The king was sitting on his royal throne in the hall, facing the entrance. When he saw Queen Esther standing in the court, he was pleased with her and held out to her the gold scepter that was in his hand. So Esther approached and touched the tip of the scepter" (Esth. 5:1–2).

Sometimes the answer God provides is *you*.

To make a complicated story very short and sweet, the king listened to Esther and reversed the edict. Esther's courage met with the king's favor, and God preserved His people through her brave and resolute decision.

Esther doesn't hide and hope that God will answer her prayer, some way, somehow. She doesn't wait for a sign. She doesn't ask for permission. She doesn't wait for someone else to make a move first.

She moves.

She acts.

She goes.

She speaks.

She takes a chance.

She stands firm.

She believes she can be used by God.

Sometimes the answer to an overwhelming situation isn't a big miracle or God's direct and supernatural intervention. Sometimes the answer God provides is *you*. The biggest miracle of all is that God lets *you* be the answer.

DISCOVERING YOUR PLACE

The pro-life movement needs more voices. We need defenders of the unborn and protectors of the mommas who carry them.

We need people who will move, act, go, and speak.

The March for Life is an annual gathering when thousands of pro-life demonstrators flood the National Mall in Washington, DC, on or near January 22, the anniversary of the 1973 Supreme Court decision that allowed abortion to be legalized throughout the United States. You may have heard about it, although the media doesn't give it the attention it deserves.

When our Embrace Grace team made the decision to go to the March for Life for the first time, we were excited and expected to stand out as the "loving" organization. We had made signs that had sayings like, *Be strong. I will never leave or give up on your life. I am with you always—God* and *Don't Worry. I will care for your every need.—God.* We thought that with our love we were going to stick out among a sea of angry people. But we were so wrong.

Everyone was full of love!

All the signs were beautiful and heartfelt. The participants at the March for Life were amazing, and we felt strong and unified by being there all together. We were all there to march on behalf of lives that need protection.

Please consider attending the national March for Life at least once! If you can't make it to the DC March, you might be able to join the statewide march at your state capitol. It's important we continue to show up and maintain our solidarity and power as a pro-life movement.

Even if you cannot attend a rally or demonstration in person, please do not ignore the opportunity at your fingertips. The power of social media is hard not to recognize. It goes far beyond just staying in touch with friends and sharing photos and jokes. The Internet is also a force for societal change that shines a light on causes worth our time and attention. Social media channels empower the world to unite and bring change in the pro-life movement. If used in the best way, social media can connect people, organize our efforts, and communicate a pro-life—and *pro-love*—message to the world.

Obedience pleases the One who matters most: God.

Be aware that standing up for a message like this one, whether through a public gathering or through sharing posts online, may come with a painful pricetag. Some friends and family may openly question you or distance themselves without commentary. It's difficult to take a stand for God's truth if we are worried about what people think about us. When we make our decisions based on what other people think, we let them control us. We waste time and energy trying to figure out who other people want us to be. The more energy we spend trying not to offend others, the more vulnerable we are to cave into criticism.

We have to be okay knowing we can't please everyone—that it's *impossible* to please everyone. Obedience pleases the One who matters most: God. Our voices matter and have influence. Every time you write on your blog, upload your podcast, and share those pro-life articles, you are changing the world!

We need people of courage to stand up to evil in a culture that's saying what's wrong is right and twisting darkness into light.

WHAT PROTECTING HER CAN LOOK LIKE

Lauren McAfee is the granddaughter of the founder of Hobby Lobby, David Green, and the daughter of the president of Hobby Lobby, Steve Green. She is also a good friend and an amazing advocate for life, using her influence and voice to help save lives.

Lauren's influential family made pro-life headlines in 2014 when their case made it to the Supreme Court.[1] At issue in Burwell vs. Hobby Lobby was the Health and Human Service (HHS) Mandate that would have required David and Barbara Green and their family business to provide and facilitate four potentially life-terminating drugs and devices in their health insurance plan or pay severe fines. The Greens argued that the mandate substantially burdened their religious beliefs and stood in violation of a federal law, the Religious Freedom Restoration Act.

The Supreme Court granted a landmark victory for religious liberty on June 30, 2014, ruling that individuals do not lose their religious freedom when they open a family business. The court ruled 5-4 in favor of David and Barbara Green and Hobby Lobby, ruling that they do not have to violate their faith or pay severe fines.

Lauren and the Green family were encouraged to see so many people praying outside the Supreme Court and rallying for them. They were in a fight for the lives of the unborn, and the people who showed up to support them were the fuel they needed to keep going. Lauren said,

> During Hobby Lobby's case we had an amazing section of "cheerleaders" outside the Supreme Court all morning. We remember walking out of the court and down the Supreme Court steps to the media interviews right outside, and we could hear the pro-life activists cheering for us. It made us all smile, and I remember my grandma giving them a thumbs up to thank them for their support. We were too far away to interact, but it was a small way of thanking them. There were of course activists on the opposite side of the issue as well, who were chanting their own things against us, but there were fewer of them. Concerned Women of America, the Alliance Defending Freedom, and Becket Law were some of the groups who coordinated the cheering section for our case. It definitely gave us courage.
>
> Then for the Little Sisters of the Poor Supreme Court case [another HHS Mandate case],[2] which was also a pro-life focus, I was able to be among the supporters. I was in the cheering section outside the Supreme Court during their oral argument. I gave a short speech, along with many others outside and cheered them on when they came out of their oral argument. It is a nice way to support people going through a court/legal case. When

you are going through it, it is scary, and you never know how things are going to turn out. Having others visibly support you is really encouraging.

If you are embarking on a new career path, pray about being an attorney who defends life and religious liberties or one who helps single moms navigate messy custody battles. You can give your time to be an oasis of peace during a stressful season for her.

Consider pursuing becoming a politician who not only stands for life and godly values but who has a pro-life perspective to support policies that empower all races and ages of women at every socio-economic level to have peace in knowing they can have their baby and their dreams too.

Consider a career as a pro-life doctor or other medical professional who will support women and families who choose life, even when the baby they are carrying has a terminal illness.

What if you are not called to lean into one of these careers? You can encourage those who are. Gather in support outside courthouses, thank your legislators who take a pro-life stance, and vote, vote, vote. We all need to be voting for and supporting pro-life politicians. Your notes, calls, and emails of encouragement make a difference. So many attorneys and legislators say they only ever get angry calls, when people don't like their decisions. They are so encouraged by calls, emails, and social media posts thanking them for taking a stand for life.

There are endless ways you can protect and defend the powerless. Whether you use your voice on a large stage, on social media, or just in conversation with one person, you are making a difference.

We recently had a young woman named Allie who reached out to us. She had just found out she was pregnant and was distraught and terrified. She already had one baby her parents were raising because she was having a hard time getting her life together and staying clean. When she realized she was expecting again, she reached out to the Embrace Grace team for counsel. She needed someone to talk to and process everything, but she let us know she had scheduled an abortion for the following day. Our entire Embrace Grace team rallied in prayer while my co-worker and I called and texted her throughout the day.

Her emotions were so up and down. She was feeling confident to choose life in one moment, but in the next she felt she must go through with the abortion.

Allie texted our team about her amazing experience encountering a pro-life advocate when she wasn't expecting it:

> I left the clinic, and I looked up to heaven and said, "God, give me peace on a decision. I don't know what to do." My friend reminded me that seeing the baby on the sonogram machine was a beautiful sign to choose life. But I really needed God to give me a clearer message.
>
> Later that day, on top of all my current problems, I realized a tire on my car was flat. I aired it up enough to make it to the tire shop so they could check it out. They told me it would be at least half an hour before they had an answer, so I sat in the waiting room, thinking about how my life has turned out to be a mess. While I was sitting there, I received a text from my boyfriend. He told me that our relationship was over and he didn't want to be with

me anymore. This just all felt too much.

I started crying in the waiting room. I couldn't contain my emotions. I was so scared. At that moment, a woman who was also waiting for her car came over and sat next to me. We were the only two people in the room. The first thing I noticed was that she was wearing a shirt that said *Faith Over Fear*. I didn't want to tell her what was going on but more than anything, I knew I needed prayer. I said, "Will you just pray for me? I'd rather not talk about why." I really didn't want to tell her everything going on and then just hear her say, "Choose life. Don't have an abortion."

She prayed for me, and then she paused for a few minutes as the worship music was playing. I was still crying, desperate for a sign from God to know that I would be okay if I had this baby.

She began peacefully humming the song "It Is Well" so beautifully and peacefully. After a few minutes, she began to pray again. She said, "This is not me, but the Holy Spirit has a message for you: God wants you to keep this baby."

My jaw dropped. How could she have known I was pregnant? I never said a word about it. She told me how she had an unplanned pregnancy when she was sixteen years old and almost had an abortion. She ended up choosing life and has a son and beautiful grandkids.

She continued, "Friend, God is not going to leave you now. Even when it feels like there's no way, He is a Waymaker. He is in the business of miracles. He will open doors that you won't even believe. If you would just open up your heart and receive Jesus like never before, He will blow your mind. I keep hearing the Lord say you have a king in your belly. Don't discard it. I would dare not ever say something like that on my own. God is in love with your little one."

As Allie texted us about this God-ordained appointment, our team felt in awe and full of hope. This woman in a tire shop waiting room was hearing directly from the Lord and using her voice to advocate for the "king" in Allie's belly.

Our team reached out to see who could help. Some of our staff committed to reimbursing her for any payment Allie had already made to the abortion clinic. Someone offered a room in her home for Allie to live in. Others offered to cover her baby gifts or anything she might need. It was beautiful to see amazing advocates using their voices and resources to help save a life, even a stranger in a tire shop.

Working in the pro-life movement is not for the weak at heart. There are amazing and miraculous moments that make our hearts burst with joy and gratitude. The life decisions we witness and the glory stories we hear become the fuel that keeps us dedicated to the cause. Stories of lives saved and transformed are forever my favorite.

But then there are the moments that make our hearts fall into our stomachs while tears roll down our cheeks. We grieve every loss of life. It's hard when we put everything on the line to help empower a mom to choose life, but she can't look away from the fear long enough to see God's hand right in front of her. I wish I could say that the girl in the story I just shared chose life and everything worked out, but she didn't. With all the confirmations sent from heaven that God would take care of her and her child, Allie still chose to go through with the abortion.

As we serve these mommas, we have to remember that it is our job to be obedient and God's job to orchestrate everything else. We are not a savior. We are walking reminders of God's faithfulness and love to a world that needs hope. Even if a young mom chooses fear over faith, we still need to care for her and help point her to healing.

Don't give up when it gets hard. This kind of ministry can be messy sometimes, those are just the times when we need to rely all the more on our Messiah. We know that for those of us who love God, all things work together for good. Even though it grieves His heart, He is never taken by surprise when a mom makes a decision to abort. He loves her all the same. We must not grow weary in doing good. Experiencing loss makes the joy we have when a life decision is made even greater. It's the glimpses of glory that fuel our passion to serve.

Jesus said, "Did I not tell you that if you believe, you will see the glory of God?" (John 11:40). Don't stop using your voice, your resources, and your love to stand up for moms who need help being brave. We need you in the pro-life movement. Be strong and courageous—and believe.

Ideas for How to Protect Her

- When January rolls around each year, pray for those at the March for Life in Washington, DC, and attend in person, if you can. If you can't make that one, attend the march in your state. Bring your kids and extended families. The bigger the presence, the bigger the impact!

- Pray for, donate to, and use your voice to support pro-life legal organizations representing cases that defend the sanctity of life.

- Attorneys, the pro-life movement needs your help. Donate a few hours per month to help single moms navigate custody issues or offer a virtual class for single moms to answer their frequently asked questions.

- Run for office! The best way to make the law more pro-life is to develop more pro-life lawmakers.

- Attend local pro-life rallies in your area throughout the year.

- Do you know you're pro-life but clam up when someone challenges you on why you believe what you believe? Take a training course with organizations like Equal Rights Institute or Life Training Institute to learn to have healthy and informed dialogue that inspires change.

- Maybe you know about the apologetics of why abortion is WRONG but are struggling with the grace that Scripture outlines for women with unplanned pregnancies. Or maybe you want to talk about the issue without bringing up politics. Pro-Grace is an awesome training organization for how to have these discussions and how to turn the tide of abortion through God's grace.

- Do you have a substantial social media following? Be a brand ambassador for your favorite pro-life organization and help them grow. Share their posts, wear their swag, and give a call to action for people to get involved.

- Live Action has the largest pro-life online presence, reaching millions of people through their daily news. Sign up to have their news delivered daily to your inbox so you can stay up to date and have articles, fact sheets, videos, and graphics to use your voice and platform to save lives.

- Lobby to change the laws, both at the federal and state level.

- Connect with the National Right to Life and your state Right to Life to learn how you can elect pro-life candidates and help pass state and federal pro-life laws.

- Don't forget to vote and support pro-life candidates. If you're not sure where your candidate stands on pro-life issues, check out My Faith Votes or the Susan B. Anthony List.

- Share pro-life memes and graphics on your social media. Create your own, share other organizations', or grab amazing memes for free from The Radiance Foundation!

- Attend legal rallies at courts during pro-life cases to show support.

- Send a pro-life message to your elected leaders.

- Invite your friends over to watch the movie *Unplanned*, a scripted film that tells the real-life story of Abby Johnson, the former director of a Planned Parenthood clinic who became an anti-abortion activist.

- Learn the facts about abortion in the United States to be able to articulate and argue against abortion. Facts can change hearts. Abort73 provides comprehensive information and statistics.

- Thank legislators who take a pro-life stand. Stand out from the complaints and negativity many legislators face daily by just calling to say thank you.

- Share your story! Whether it's with one person, on your social media, or on a stage, be bold in sharing your unplanned pregnancy story, adoption story, or abortion story. Your story can help heal others and inspire them to be bold in sharing theirs too!

- Wear pro-life gear that sparks conversations. Many organizations sell merchandise with inspiring messaging, and your purchase helps support their pro-life cause.

- Students, get involved in your school or university's Students for Life group. If there isn't one, then start one! They recruit, train, and mobilize students to abolish abortion.

- Handwrite "Dear Brave Girl" letters to be placed inside the Love Boxes given to women with unplanned pregnancies. You get to speak life into the lives of women who have recently found out they were pregnant. You can find the letter download link and instructions on the Embrace Grace website.

- Support and give to ministries that fight for religious liberties and sanctity of life by funding cases, training attorneys, and successfully advocating for freedom, such as the Alliance Defending Freedom.

- Employers, review your maternity benefits. Look for ways to develop a pro-family approach and culture in your companies to provide ample time off for new parents to recover and bond with their child as well as compensation for maternity leave. These workplace supports can inspire a life decision. No woman should have to feel like she has to choose between her child or her job. For ideas on appropriate time to be given for maternity leave, connect with Families Valued.

- Do you know a student with an unplanned pregnancy who is being treated unfairly by the university, perhaps losing a scholarship or being forced to move out of her dorm room? Check out the Pregnant on Campus Initiative by Students for Life to find out what her rights are.

- Women can't access abortions if there are no workers to staff the clinics. Get connected to And Then There Were None to help abortion clinic workers leave the abortion industry. They are devoted to end abortion from the inside out! Clinic worker's lives are valuable too and this ministry supports them through the transition process of jobs and helps them on their healing journey for as long as needed. Get connected and see how you can get involved.

- Talk with your kids about what it means to be pro-life and give them words of encouragement to use if they encounter a friend who unexpectedly finds out she is pregnant.

National Organizations to Serve and Support

Abort73	abort73.com
And Then There Were None	abortionworker.com
Alliance Defending Freedom	adflegal.org
Embrace Grace Love Box Initiative	EmbraceGrace.com
Equal Rights Institute	equalrightsinstitute.com
Families Valued	familiesvalued.org
Life Training Institute	prolifetraining.com
Live Action	liveaction.org
March for Life	marchforlife.org
My Faith Votes	myfaithvotes.org
National Right to Life	nrlc.org
Pro-Grace	prograce.org
Radiance Foundation	theradiancefoundation.org
Students for Life	studentsforlife.org
Susan B. Anthony List	sba-list.org

5

LOVE HER

Creating a Safe Place for Inner Healing

One hot Texas summer day, all four of my kids were craving a Sonic slush to cool off. Seeing their red and sweaty faces in the back seat of the car, I couldn't say no. We drove to Sonic and ordered our drinks, and when I opened my wallet to pull out cash, I didn't have any! I only had a credit card. I prefer to pay with cash at Sonic. We've had Embrace Grace moms who work at Sonic make comments about people not tipping sometimes. I try to make sure I have cash because if you swipe a card, there isn't a tip line to fill out. If you don't have cash, you can't tip.

Reluctantly I swiped my card and waited. The young waitress came out just a few minutes later, balancing all of our slushies on her red tray. I preemptively said, "I'm so sorry, but I thought I had cash in my purse to tip you. My bank is just right around the corner. I'll go grab some cash for a tip and come back and bring it to you."

She answered with a smile, "Oh no, you don't have to do that. . . . But if you want to, you can. I'll be here."

So I did. I zipped over to the bank and withdrew enough cash to tip her. When I came back to give it to her, she seemed excited.

Her smile was contagious. I couldn't help asking her name.

"Zoe," she answered.

I lit up excitedly. "I *love* that name! I have a baby boy named Judah, but before I knew he was a boy, I had picked Zoe as an option if my baby was a girl. Did you know your name means *life*? But not just any kind of life. It's not just a survival type of life— it's more of a heavenly-realm type of life. It's the kind of life that Jesus paid a price for us to have—an abundant and eternal life. Did you know that?"

She stammered, "Ummm no . . . so, umm, you have a baby?"

I thought she would be excited about the meaning of her name, but she seemed more interested in my baby.

"Yeah," I responded. "He's getting to be a big baby. He's a little over one year old now."

She looked at me and said, "Do you have any advice for me? Me and my boyfriend just found out we are expecting, and we are trying to just figure out what this is going to look like."

What a divine moment! God brought her to me, and all I thought I was doing was stopping for some slushies.

Zoe and I exchanged info, and she got connected to an Embrace Grace group. Later, I was in the audience at her wedding. Then I got to celebrate the birth of her sweet son. Her husband even worked for my husband for a while.

A tremendous connection began with a simple question: "What's your name?"

That question comprised more than just small talk. It was the beginning of the Holy Spirit's invitation to allow God to shower her with love and begin healing to her heart.

Zoe says, "At the time, I took everything Embrace Grace did for me for granted. A girl who was only 'half in' was loved and cherished, and had blessings poured upon her like all the others who were 'all in.' Because that's what God called them to do, because they obeyed Him and planted seeds, I was able to see Him through it all years later. He was working in my life through these women and this group, even when I didn't notice. I'm so thankful for Him and His overall plan for my life. Honestly, I don't know where my life would have gone if I didn't have my sweet firstborn. God really used him to turn me around. Over and over, in everything I was doing during this journey into motherhood, God was pointing me back to Him. Even in the midst of this unplanned pregnancy, God had a plan. He was so patient with me, and I couldn't see any of it until I was on the other side of the healing. It's amazing how He shows up in little ways, like in a conversation with a sweet woman during your shift at Sonic, or that sweet tiny baby who's the size of a sesame seed."

WHAT THE BIBLE HAS TO SAY ABOUT INNER HEALING

Because I have four kids, I've been to plenty of doctor visits over the years. I'm thankful it's mostly been for minor issues like colds, flu, ear infections, and stomach bugs. In every visit, I want to know what is wrong and how my child can be healthy again. The doctor asks about symptoms, does testing and scans, and then finds the root of the problem before determining a plan for healing.

In the same way, single and pregnant women everywhere are struggling with emotions that need healing. They've been through hard, damaging experiences that need to be brought out into the open for God to heal in safe environments through safe people. Many mommas struggle with depression, anger, detachment, isolation, bitterness, frustration, and fear. A lot of that pain is caused by abandonment, different forms of abuse, broken trust, mother and father wounds, rejection, a lack of community, and a sense of hopelessness. It's easy to ignore the pain, run from it, try to forget it, blame others for it, or cover it up because it hurts too much to look closely at pain. But if we can help these moms heal, they will parent from a place of wholeness and emotional health.

The health of our hearts determines the quality of our lives.

At times, the church tends to focus on the symptoms of sin instead of helping a mom uncover root causes of the pain. God wants to go straight to the heart of the problem with a prescription. In the book of Proverbs we learn that the root of any problem is always in the heart: "Above all else, guard your heart, for everything you do flows from it" (4:23). The health of our hearts determines the quality of our lives.

Physical pain may only take days or weeks to heal. If we cut an arm, receive stitches, or break a bone, we know healing will happen in the near future. But with emotional pain, sometimes it can take a lot longer, it's not something we can just put a bandage on and hope. Things may get worse before they get better, requiring a bit of heart surgery by opening up our deepest selves and allowing God to heal. Psalm 147:3 says, "He heals the brokenhearted and binds up their wounds."

As the church, we can facilitate a safe place for mommas to reveal the inner hurt she's been carrying and help her forgive and release those who have hurt her. We can help her learn how to replace negative thoughts and the enemy's lies with God's truth. Only then can she look up and see that the future is good.

A lot of times we may be limited in our knowledge of how to help someone heal, and we need to connect them to professional, licensed counselors. We should always be looking for warning signs that a professional is needed. This is always the case with a violent relationship, self-cutting, or suicidal thoughts. But as the church, we can make sure she doesn't feel alone as she finds the root of her pain. There is nothing like seeing a woman come to understand that she is more than her past mistakes or the lies she has believed about herself and that she is passionately loved by Jesus.

DISCOVERING YOUR PLACE

If you want to help others heal, look for the many ways you might serve in the pro-life movement. Perhaps you have been the recipient of healing prayer and have experienced God move powerfully in your own life. You may have a passion to see people set free, healed, and delivered. Perhaps the very way God healed your heart is the way He wants to heal others through you.

Start somewhere. Start *anywhere*. God will show you how to love her.

New dads and moms need healing. The parents of those who have experienced an unplanned pregnancy may need healing. Birth moms who place their baby for adoption need healing. Children in the foster care system need healing. Women who suffer loss through miscarriage need healing.

You can use the gifts God placed in you to lead others to healing through mentoring, leading a small group, or just being a friend. Start somewhere. Start *anywhere*. God will show you how to love her.

While men can of course be essential influencers in many aspects of living out our commitment to preserve and protect life, women are usually the best choice to come alongside single and pregnant young mothers to empathize, help, and mentor them through healing from such personal hurts and traumatic experiences.

WHAT LOVING HER CAN LOOK LIKE

I recently heard of a beautiful organization called Abel Speaks that helps women and families who have chosen to carry a child with a life-limiting diagnosis. Many times when a woman finds out she has a child with a terminal illness, health professionals try to persuade her to terminate the pregnancy. Many women who receive positive test results for an abnormality will terminate the pregnancy. Some doctors will determine the diagnosis is a helpless cause and make it difficult to find a team of professionals who will help medically and emotionally.

Abel Speaks not only provides empathy and understanding

through mentorship for those experiencing loss like this, but also connects them to pro-life doctors and community as well as birth support with a doula, maternity and birth photographer, and a beautiful keepsake memory box. Community is vital to healing for a mom who may be walking through a pregnancy that will eventually deliver a child who may only live moments, hours, or a few days.

It brings all of us great sorrow when some moms with unplanned pregnancies finally get through the initial fear of finding out about her pregnancy only to come to an earth-shattering moment when the baby no longer has a heartbeat. The pain and trauma of pregnancy loss can cause a young mom to spiral down into a world of grief. She will experience a roller coaster of emotions, and it's unbearable for her to process the grief alone. She had fully accepted the changes and challenges that come with carrying a life—and then it went away. Some mommas try to fill the immediate void caused by loss by trying to get pregnant again, thinking it will ease the pain. What she really needs is a mentor and friend who can help her fill the void with the love of God. Loving her through her healing process is a beautiful way to serve.

We once had an Embrace Grace mom who unexpectedly lost her baby at twenty weeks. We were almost to the end of the semester, and she was emotionally connected to each of the moms in the group. The loss of her baby was devastating for her and for the other pregnant moms. We knew it would be hard for her to attend Princess Day. Her grieving heart was fragile. We knew it was best to wait a few weeks, and then hold a unique Princess Day just for her. Someone came and did her hair and make-up.

We served a beautiful meal for her, and we set up a memorial table for her baby. We bought gifts that would help her always remember her sweet baby girl. We enjoyed each other's company in a special way that evening. It was an event that she still talks about today as a day that touched her heart forever.

Embrace Grace is a helpful beginning to the healing process in a single and pregnant mom's heart. Anyone can lead an Embrace Grace group because the curriculum is presented in a digital format, featuring pastors, counselors, our team, and other mommas who share testimonials that will encourage and inspire. Online training and a supportive team at the national offices help every Embrace Grace group be successful in helping moms heal. The program covers topics like salvation, identity, faith, God's Word, sin, forgiveness, repentance, and grace.

A key component of the curriculum in Embrace Grace is a special night we call "Breaking Chains Night." After a few weeks in the group, the moms are starting to let their walls down, and they realize it is an atmosphere where it is safe to share their hurt and pain.

On Breaking Chains night, we pair each mom with two leaders and guide her through an exercise of writing down the invisible chains that have been holding her back and weighing her down. Those chains might be unforgiveness, guilt, rejection, abandonment, and on and on. When she is finished, we ask her if she's ready to lay it all at the foot of the cross. A few moms answer no; their hearts are still so tender and unready to release the pain quite just yet. But many *are* ready. It is miraculous to see tears of release flow down her face, as her vacant stare changes to hope shining through her countenance. After she has released her pain, we give each mom a cuff bracelet that says Free, to symbolize that her chains have been broken and she's been set free. It's unforgettable to watch a single and pregnant mom go from feeling like an orphan to a daughter of the King.

I love the way Pastor Hernandez in Pasadena, Texas, helps others heal by blessing the single and pregnant moms at his church. He told me once how he gives his children a Father's Blessing every night before they go to bed, and how it broke his heart that many of these moms have probably never received something like that from their fathers. So he spends time in prayer and shows up on Princess Day with a special word for the moms. He prays a unique Father's Blessing over each one of them. He sent me one he wrote for a single and pregnant Christian mom named Kelci:

> Today, Kelci, I will crown you as a representation of the princess you are in the sight of God and in the presence of everyone here. This also represents the crown you receive when God greets you in heaven and rewards you for your steadfast faith and trust in Him when life became uncertain. As you follow after Him and allow Him to lead you and your family's life, you will receive the crown of blessing (Prov. 10:6). . . .
>
> There are a few things every little girl should hear from a father. And I would like to speak those to you now.
>
> I am proud of you. You are beautiful inside and out. You are special. You are perfect just the way you are. I believe in you. You are wonderful. God knows what you

have gone through—your hurts, pains, disappointments, the fears you carry.

Now I will pronounce a blessing over you and your family's life. Abraham was blessed by God in the Bible, and that blessing flowed and continues for generations. Today you will receive that blessing.

Kelci, may God bless you, look over you, and protect you. May He keep you safe from harm and bring comfort to you in times of uncertainty. May God shine His face toward you and love you with an everlasting love that will not fail you, reject you, or let you down. May God's presence surround you and your family and bring peace to your life and in your home. Amen.

Ideas for How to Love Her

- Be willing to share your own story—even the messy parts. Tell how God has helped begin the healing process in areas of your life where you needed it. The more vulnerable you are, the more open she will feel when sharing her own struggles.

- Sponsor her to attend a women's retreat or conference to encourage her. There are ministry events all over the nation and world. She will have affirmation of her true identity, build meaningful relationships, and develop a fresh perspective of her purpose with a renewed passion for life!

- See if your local college has Christian counselors majoring in psychology who would want to counsel her through the church or local pregnancy center for their practicum.

- Ask your church if they can set aside funds to cover the cost of a single and pregnant mom to receive professional counseling, or ask a counselor if she might donate a few hours per month to address special needs that arise within the church for single and pregnant women.

- Help her forgive someone. If she seems to have a lot of bitterness toward someone, like a parent or the father of her baby, help her understand forgiveness and how to release hurts so that she can move ahead emotionally and mentally lighter. Forgiving someone will allow her to function better in every aspect of her life. One way might be to have her write a letter of forgiveness to someone who has hurt her. She may not ever mail the letter, but the act of writing out the hurt and the statement of forgiveness can be healing.

- Get her connected to an Embrace Grace group for discipleship and inner heart healing during her pregnancy. If your church doesn't have a group, consider starting one.

- If she has experienced sexual abuse, trauma, or confusion, help connect her to a counselor who can talk it through safely. A great companion resource for her as she walks through her healing journey is a book called *Love & Sex* by Nancy Houston or *Surprised by the Healer* by Linda Dillow and Dr. Juli Slattery.

- Start a Mending the Soul group at your church. Mending the Soul provides curriculum and resources that walk survivors of abuse and trauma through the healing process gently and holistically. They provide materials for small group connection and training for leaders to facilitate healing from the inside out.

- Connection and having fun heals the heart too! All of us have an amazing ministry opportunity to lovingly create a sense of belonging to moms who are struggling with loneliness and depression.

- If a mom is struggling with addiction, look for a Celebrate Recovery Group, at your church or another church. Celebrate Recovery is a faith-based support group for all types of addictions. If you can't find one, ask around and see if someone you know would want to start one at your church.

- Ask your church to offer more topical classes that cover issues many single and pregnant moms face, such as rejection, abandonment, mother/father wounds, grief, and depression. We need freedom ministry, any ministry that pertains to mental and emotional help. A great resource to check out is Unlocked Ministries.

- Many moms who marry someone other than the father of the baby have to navigate how to blend families with unity. Many churches don't offer a resource or class to help blended families heal and work together in oneness with Christ. Check out Blended Kingdom Families as an amazing resource for her and for your church.

- Be present when someone is pouring their heart out to you. Always make the person in front of you (or on the phone) the most important person in that moment. It takes great bravery and courage for her to share what she's feeling and going through. Be a listening ear and comfort for her.

• Create an atmosphere where you recognize the presence of the Holy Spirit as you spend time with her, either in a group format or one-on-one. Whether or not a woman is receiving help from a Christian counselor, she may make significant strides forward in her healing through those shared moments in God's presence.

• Look past the symptoms of her pain and help her get to the root of her pain. Ask questions, and allow the Holy Spirit to guide the discussion. Once the root is revealed, consider next steps—forgiveness to be given or received, counseling through church or professionals, or seeking God's truth to replace a lie she has believed about herself.

• Watch for moms in abusive relationships and those struggling with eating disorders, cutting, suicidal thoughts, or depression. Help connect her to a counselor or support systems that specialize with her particular struggle.

Helping after Infant Loss or Pregnancy Loss

There is nothing you can buy that can take the pain away altogether, but acts of love and compassion can help the grieving process and remind a grieving mother that she is not alone.

• Be present and stay committed for the long-term. Check in regularly with compassion and support.

- Send a card or text of encouragement. Make it personal and real. She needs to know you care about her and the baby she lost.

- Bring her a meal and give her a hug. Just sit and listen. You don't have to fix anything because you can't. Just listen and love.

- Buy her groceries or have them delivered. Find out her favorite foods and let her rest while you take a trip to the grocery store.

- Donate to a pro-life charity in memory of the baby. Have them send a note of acknowledgment to her that the donation was made in her child's honor.

- Help cover funeral expenses for the baby. Most single moms don't have the extra money to cover the cost of honoring the life that has been lost. Ask your church to host the funeral and provide a pastor to officiate.

- Send flowers—yellow or pink for a girl and blue, green, or white for a boy. Little touches and thoughtful gestures mean so much to a momma grieving.

- Offer to do laundry or babysit her children if she has another child. A break from chores or childcare for a few hours or a few days allows the time for needed rest.

- Connect her to an infant loss support group at your church when the time is appropriate. If you don't have one, pray about starting one or introduce her to someone who has been through a similar loss.

- Give a gift that helps with her healing, such as a book, a devotional, or a special healing box offered through infant loss ministries like Hope Mommies and I Am Fruitful.

- Depending how far along she was in her pregnancy when she lost her baby, her body may need significant physical healing to get back to full health. Do what you can to help her relax and stay off her feet as much as possible as she heals. Clean her house. Run her errands.

- Help make returns for her for both maternity clothing and baby items she doesn't want to keep. She may want to keep some because of emotional ties. But it may be easier for her to let you donate items she doesn't want to keep to a local charity.

- Give a gift that helps her remember her baby—maybe jewelry with her child's name or initial engraved, an engraved keepsake box where she can preserve sonogram photos and other items that remind her of the baby, or a quilt made from baby blankets she had collected.

- Grieve with her on important days like the anniversary of the day the child passed away or day the baby would have been due. Set a reminder in your calendar to connect with her in some way by a card, text, phone call, or lunch.

- If she finds out her baby has a terminal illness, help her connect with a pro-life doctor who will be an encouragement and value her life and the unborn baby's life. Find a local organization that will support her during the pregnancy and after.

Check out Abel Speaks, an organization that supports families that choose to carry a child with a life-limiting diagnosis.

- Send her a gift card to a local spa for a day of pampering. Even if it feels too soon after the loss, she will go when she's ready. Time to take a deep breath and relax can help her heart, too.

- Honor her baby publicly by name through a social media post. Show that her baby matters, and allow others to lift her up in prayer.

- Write a card to her baby for her to open on her due date. Share how much that unborn child is loved and missed dearly. It is beautiful for her to see and hear other people love her baby even in the baby's absence.

National Organizations to Serve and Support

Abel Speaks	abelspeaks.org
Blended Kingdom Families	blendedkingdomfamilies.com
Celebrate Recovery	celebraterecovery.com
Embrace Grace	embracegrace.com
Hope Mommies	hopemommies.org
I Am Fruitful	iamfruitful.org
Mending the Soul	mendingthesoul.org
The Quest Life	thequestlife.com
Unlocked Ministries	iamunlocked.org

SUPPORT HER

Being There for the Ones Who Choose Adoption

A group of about eight men and women gathered in a conference room at Embrace Grace headquarters to strategize about how to show more of the *love* in the pro-life (*pro-love*) movement. At the end of the meeting, we went around the room to share our passion about the cause for life.

We were spellbound when Danielle started to tell her story.

She explained that more than fifty years earlier she'd had an unplanned pregnancy. Tears flowed as she talked about the shame she carried during that season in her young life. As soon as they learned she was pregnant, Danielle's parents told her she could not and *would not* bring embarrassment to the family because of what she had done. They sent her to another city, telling everyone they knew, including her siblings, that she was going to an exclusive dance school in New York. In reality, she lived at a maternity home. Her parents went to such extreme measures to hide their daughter's predicament they used a fake name. They wanted to make sure news of her pregnancy would never leak beyond the walls of the maternity home.

The scheme was elaborate. When a friend wanted to write to Danielle, her parents gave them the address of the dance school, where a dancer had agreed to accept the letters and send them on to the maternity home. That meant when it was time to write back, Danielle sent correspondence to the dancer so she could then mail the letters with a postmark from New York.

With her identity taken this way, Danielle sat alone night after night, terrified for her future. It was too easy to believe the lie that she had ruined her life forever and would never be good enough to be accepted in her own family. Eventually, Danielle chose adoption because she felt it was the only option she had.

In the meeting that day, we all wept with Danielle. Her grief over that period of isolation, now half-a-century old, had not faded.

But as she continued her story, both her tears and ours turned into genuine smiles as she reflected on having recently found her biological daughter, Christie. These days, Christie and Danielle talk often, and Christie thinks highly of her birth mother. Christie considers Danielle brave for going through all she did to choose life. Christie has had a great life and is thankful for that gift.

When Danielle finished her story and wiped her tears, her face was glowing. God had restored a sense of blessing around the experience of pregnancy, which had been so painful at the time.

As we listened, it seemed right to tell her about the Princess Day in the Embrace Grace program. She needed to know that we are committed to a better way at Embrace Grace. Single and pregnant mommas who go through our curriculum are crowned and told of God's great love for them. They are called to come forward in their true identity and be seen for who God created them to be. These practices are a far cry from the drastic measures of the past, when girls like Danielle were hidden from society.

Danielle looked at me in wonder as I shared about this part of our program. Tears filled her eyes again as she said, "You know, if someone had put a crown on my head, that would have changed everything. *Everything.*"

Yes, identity is *everything*.

If we believe one thing at Embrace Grace, it is that it's never too late. So we did what anyone would have done in that moment. Right in the middle of that business meeting, we ran down the hall to grab a tiara. When we placed it on her head, we looked in her eyes and told her how brave and courageous she was for choosing life fifty years ago. We told her she is a hero. She'd had to wait too long to hear those words, longer than anyone should have to.

When Danielle left our office at the end of the meeting, we watched her walk out of the building, get into her car, and drive away.

She never took off her crown.

That's the power of identity. Knowing *who we are* and *Whose we are* truly changes *everything*.

WHAT THE BIBLE HAS TO SAY
ABOUT ADOPTION

I enjoy the various relationships I have with Embrace Grace moms. Many of them bravely choose to parent, but sometimes I have had the honor to walk alongside a birth mom who chooses adoption, a mom who carries life within her to bless another family. Every time I do, it changes me. I am intensely moved by every detail. It is captivating to watch God bring together two families with the same hearts and then there is a beautiful exchange. To transfer one life into the care of someone else, to entrust your most valuable gift to another person, is humbling to see. I am in awe of a mother who would invite another family to provide her baby with a life she could not have provided herself. When she chooses adoption, a birth mother becomes an answered prayer for someone who may have prayed her whole life for a child of her own.

It is one thing to witness the act of love a birth mom makes, rejecting abortion and sacrificing her body for nine months to save a baby's life. But then it is breathtaking to see an adoptive mom open her family, heart, and home to love and raise a baby as though he or she came from her own womb.

As I have walked through the adoption journey with some of the Embrace Grace moms, God has shown me how He sees adoption.

Exodus 1 and 2 describe how God had blessed the Israelites with many babies and their population had grown rapidly. The Egyptian pharaoh feels threatened by their numbers and worries that the Israelites could overtake his throne. He orders that all the baby boys be drowned in the Nile River. After the cruel declaration, a woman gives birth to a baby boy named Moses. She loves Moses and knows he is special.

For three months, she tries her best to take care of him; eventually, however, she realizes that hiding him won't work much longer. To save her baby's life, she has to let him go. Having kids of my own, I can hardly imagine the strength, courage, and love she must have had to release that baby. She wholeheartedly trusts God to take care of him.

The process is unconventional, to say the least. Moses's mother places him for adoption by placing him in a river, in the very river meant to drown him, in fact. She gathers all the materials to hand-make a basket just the right size for her sweet baby, patching it with tar to make it waterproof. Then she actually *does* it—releases her priceless treasure, after one more kiss, one more hug, one more prayer.

Oh God, please save my baby.

Most of us know the rest of the story. Pharaoh's daughter finds the baby in the basket and loves him immediately. But she needs a woman who can nurse the baby, and through a miraculous series of connections, Moses's birth mother is chosen to care for him. God rewards her for her obedience.

Then it becomes official. When Moses is older, Pharaoh adopts him, and he lives in Pharaoh's palace as part of their family. They treat Moses as their own.

Moses, of course, becomes the great leader of the Isrealites, through whom God performs miracles not seen before or since. He guides the Israelites out of slavery and bondage, as God's chosen leader to save the entire nation from destruction.

Moses changes the world.

But what would have happened if his birth mom had not released him and given God control? What if she just couldn't let her baby go? What if she had continued to live in hiding, determined to rear Moses herself? What kind of life would he have lived? The story would have had a much different ending.

DISCOVERING YOUR PLACE

I've had a lot of conversations with moms who are considering having an abortion, and when I bring up the option of adoption they immediately shut it down. When I ask them why, for the most part they say, "I don't know. That would just be weird. I can't give my baby away."

Twenty-plus years ago, adoption was a lot less popular than it is today. Many single and pregnant women were sent away; there were a lot of secrets. Now the adoption discussion is more open and the birth mom feels empowered in her choice of who will parent.

Until a person has walked the same roads these birth moms walk, it is hard to understand just how strong they are, how many obstacles they overcome, and how much they sacrifice for the sake of an innocent life. The truth is, birth moms are heroes, and people need to know it—especially the birth moms themselves. They don't always see themselves as champions.

Adoption isn't an easy decision or process. It comes with an aftershock of heartache. Birth moms feel isolated and lonely immediately after they have released their baby into another family's care. Some react much like a mother who experiences the death of an infant or unborn baby; there is an element of grief involved. What a birth mom needs most is someone to support her before, during, and after the process.

She needs someone to grieve with her.

One of the main reasons a girl might choose adoption is financial hardship; she may not be able to provide the life she wishes for her child. If that's the case for a mom you are mentoring or helping, start an imaginative conversation about what it might look like for her to have everything she needed. Invite her to explore the possibilities and dream out loud. What would she need financially? Would she need a better job? Would she need a car? Would she need childcare? Sometimes with a little help from a community of people, she can have her dreams and her baby, too. Some moms will choose to keep a baby because she believes that she will have the support she needs.

Other moms may choose adoption; these moms need the tools and resources to connect with an adoption agency. Adoption can give pregnant women the power to make a plan and choices in the best interest of the baby. A birth mom can pray to be matched with the perfect family, then meet them and talk with them, getting to know them on a personal level. Open adoptions are possible, in which the adoptive family corresponds through letters and pictures so the birth mom can watch her child grow.

It is always a joy to hear how birth moms find their adoptive families. Their adoption stories have a way of revealing how God has taken them on an adventure, sealing His words with amazing confirmations, showing everyone involved that adoption is part of His plan.

One particular story still moves my heart and reminds me of God's attention to detail in matching families. The birth mom had chosen an adoptive family, and they made a special agreement about the child's naming process. They decided the adoptive mom would choose the first name, but the birth mom would choose the middle name. The birth mom prayed about the middle name for a while and finally called the adoptive mom and said, "I made my decision. I would like her to have the middle name *Blair* because that's my middle name; I really want her to have something of mine."

The adoptive mom started crying and said, "That's my middle name, too!"

A sweet connection like this is not an uncommon occurrence. God tends to provide evidence of His fingerprints throughout the adoption process to give a birth mother courage and confirmation that she's making a good decision.

In a day when it has become socially acceptable to end a pregnancy out of convenience, adoption stories come as a breath of fresh air. These women have chosen to give life. Their courage should be honored. The sacrifice is great, but the reward is greater.

WHAT SUPPORTING HER CAN LOOK LIKE

BraveLove is an awesome organization that advocates for birth moms, offering options to bring them out of isolation. BraveLove helps connect birth moms to support groups and retreats all over the nation. They believe no one should walk through pregnancy alone.

Moms who have decided on adoption are included in the Embrace Grace program. Instead of a baby shower, they get a Celebration of Life Party where people at the church honor her after she places her baby for adoption. They bring gifts to honor her and her decision. They provide new clothes, gift cards, keepsakes to remind her of her baby, and more. As she passes through the wave of grief associated with adoption, she will be ready for a fresh start, so a Celebration of Life Party is the perfect way to help launch into her new beginning.

Most importantly, the church pours words of affirmation over the birth mother. There is a big bowl of beads in all different sizes, textures, and colors. Each guest at the party passes the bowl and grabs one bead that symbolizes something in the life of the birth mom, and they share about their choice. I've heard people say

> "I picked this blue bead for the color of your baby's eyes."
>
> "I picked this red bead for the sacrifice you made to save your baby's life."
>
> "I picked this pearl because through this process, you are a treasure."
>
> "I picked this clear bead because you have a pure heart."

As each bead is chosen, we add them to a necklace for her. More beautiful than the necklace is the lasting sentiment it carries. The birth mother takes home a tangible reminder that she is never alone.

Adoption is not the only time that a birth mother releases her child into the care of another family. Sometimes foster care becomes necessary. There are some moms who choose to parent, but because of their own decisions, or because of unsafe living environments, put their children in a high-risk situation or potential danger. Whether because of drugs, neglect, or abuse, Child Protective Services removes the child from the home and places him or her into the foster care system. It should always be our goal to restore the mom to a healthy place so she can receive her kids again. We can help guide her through the process of getting back on her feet practically, spiritually, and emotionally. Another way to serve is to support foster families. Both adoption and foster families have stepped in to care for children. There are beautiful ways to be a friend or to support them. One church set a congregational goal to relieve one thousand hurting children by providing foster care and adoption within a six-year time frame. They are on track to achieve this goal! Other churches keep a stock of children's clothing, furniture, and essentials so if a foster family gets an unexpected call for placement, they can quickly access what they need and provide it. Another church mobilized three hundred members to build one hundred beds for kids in foster care. Beds and cribs are one of the biggest needs for children in the foster care system.

Even businesses can donate services to foster families for a little extra support. Paul Mitchell cosmetology school in Huntsville, Alabama, hosted a free-haircut event.[1] Some YMCAs offer discounts on foster family memberships.[2] I've even heard of a local laundry service that will pick up, wash, fold, and deliver laundry. Just think of all the creative ways you can join the army of support for foster families! Even small efforts make a big difference.

An organization called America's Kids Belong offers the Dream Makers Project for kids who are aging out of the foster care system. Every year twenty-three thousand teens exit the system without a family to help them transition into adulthood. These youth were removed from their families, having experienced neglect, abuse, or abandonment, so they need support as they learn to live on their own. The Dream Makers Project draws a community around young people who have no family to help them navigate the financial challenges of young adulthood. Monumental decisions like renting an apartment, getting their first car, buying the right clothes for a new job, or locating a reasonably priced laptop for school can be overwhelming. But through the dedicated advocates in the Dream Makers Project, those milestones can be easier to reach. One young man even had a dream to become a pilot, and a donor paid for him to get his pilot's license.

Aging out of foster care on your eighteenth birthday is traumatic when you have dreamed of your own adoption story and it never materialized. Unfaulted is an organization that ministers to young people at precisely that difficult moment. Volunteers at Unfaulted reach out to girls aging out of the foster care system on or around her eighteenth birthday and give her a birthday gift. Then

The Author of Life blesses those who choose life, whether they choose parenting or adoption.

they meet with her and offer to connect her to a shepherding family willing to be a "forever family" for her. Each shepherding family has gone through extensive trauma training and committed to walking alongside this foster adult facing the prospect of navigating life without a family. Unfaulted bridges the gap and equips both parties throughout their relationship.

God is the Author of Life, and He blesses those who choose life, whether they choose parenting or adoption. There are times when you can see Him undeniably at work in an adoption story. Don't miss His fingerprints on Brandi's story, written in her own words (all names changed for privacy).

> When I was 19, I found myself with an unwanted pregnancy.... I gave my life to Christ at 16, so getting pregnant was not supposed to happen to me. I was the one who was to witness Christ to my family and see them saved! I instead saw myself as the worst sinner. Adoption was the only thing that I could think of that would make things right. I prayed for God's forgiveness and strength....
>
> God was with me all the way, and I know now that His Spirit led me. I was given a liaison with the [adoption] organization to help me if I needed anything. She also became my Lamaze coach when I went into labor.
>
> After 32 hours of labor, my daughter Macy was born. I didn't get to hear her cry and was so worried, but my liaison assured me she was healthy. I was excited for the adoptive parents, Ava and Liam, and I asked her to call them from the delivery room to tell them they had a new daughter, so she did. We all rejoiced together, and I never felt so proud, exhausted, and relieved. I finally felt like I had done something right. I asked to see her later, and a kind nurse brought her in. She was beautiful, and I was so

grateful that I did all the things they tell you to do when you're pregnant. I took care of my child for those nine months that I carried her.... It was a gift I would remember forever. Although it felt good to not be pregnant again, it also felt like a loss. So I prayed and asked Jesus to fill the void. I prayed for her, for her parents, for her extended family, and for her life. And through those prayers, I drew closer to God. I didn't know at the time how He would use this time in my life to bring me closer to Him. I rededicated my life to Jesus and started living differently.

Five years later, I got married to an amazing man and we had a daughter of our own. I was working at a bank, and life was good. I thought and prayed for my sweet Macy, that she would be happy and flourish in her family. One day, as I was working at the bank, I was organizing the vendor addresses and recognized two names from the list. They owned a restaurant in the same town. The owners' names were the parents, Ava and Liam, who adopted my daughter.... I was in shock because I couldn't deny their uncommon names. I had to find out for sure if it was them.

I called a high school friend and told her to meet me at the local restaurant the next day. We didn't know what we were doing, but God was moving. My friend began a conversation with our waitress. They knew the same people and at once I realized we were talking to the mother who adopted my daughter. I don't know how I didn't recognize her before. I said, "Do you remember me?" I introduced myself by my maiden name, and then her hands began to shake.

Ava carefully put her serving tray down and exclaimed, "We've been looking for you everywhere!" We all began to cry, and afterward she told me that Macy had always known she was adopted and was proud of it. Ava said Macy would show my senior picture to her friends, even at six years old. Ava laughed as she told us that she usually only does the books for the restaurant, but two of the waitresses called in sick that day and she was asked to help. Such a divine appointment!

As Macy grew older she began writing to me and sending me pictures. And then when she was fifteen years old, I met my daughter. She was beautiful. After that, Ava and her family included me in her life as if I was a part of their family. I was introduced at her graduation as her birth mom, and then eventually at her wedding. I was included in celebrating in the births of all three of her beautiful sons—my grandsons. My husband and I have two daughters together who know and love their older sister Macy. They all have a beautiful bond. God's love for me is so abundant!

Beauty can be born from what we never planned. Even when our lives seem messy and out of control, God may give us a glimpse of what He is doing behind the scenes. That momentary peek at

He takes our mistakes and turns them into miracles.

glory gives us the courage to keep going, knowing there are no coincidences but only Kingdom appointments.

He takes our mistakes and turns them into miracles.

Ideas for How to Support Her

For Supporting Birth Moms

- Are you a birth mom yourself and want to minister to younger birth moms? Start your own support group or mentoring program at your church to minister directly to women who have placed their baby for adoption.

- Connect her with other birth moms during her pregnancy so she can ask questions and ask advice. If you don't know of any, look for birth mom private groups on Facebook or connect with an adoption agency to see if they have a birth mom willing to share her story with a mom considering adoption during an unplanned pregnancy.

- Give her a few options of local or national adoption agencies that will support her through this season and beyond. Make sure she chooses one that feels like the best fit for her. Try an online search or connect with Catholic Charities or Lifeline Adoption Services to find birth mom support near you.

- Connect her to a birth mom support group. Check out Brave-Love for local groups, or have her ask the adoption agency she chooses whether they offer support groups.

- Help her write out her dreams and wishes for the adoptive parents and describe her hopes for what her child's adoptive family will be like. Ask her to pray over what she wrote down and that God brings the perfect family for her child.

- Celebrate Birth Mother's Day with her and provide a gift to help her feel special. National Birth Mother's Day is the Saturday before Mother's Day every year.

- Share your favorite worship songs or sermons to help keep her hopes high and focused on God throughout the pregnancy.

- Offer a safe place for her to express how she is feeling. Even if she changes her mind a million times, never persuade her. Just point her to hearing God's voice and making a decision that brings her peace. Show her how the peace of Christ can rule her heart.

- Celebrate on her milestone days after her birth. Her child's birthday will always be a special day for her, even if she can't celebrate with her baby face to face.

- Give a gift that helps her remember her baby—engraved jewelry or a keepsake box where she can keep mementos of the pregnancy, birth, and adoption.

- Help her find a private social media group for birth moms to be able to share thoughts and feelings openly with other birth moms.

- If she wants a doula to assist through the pregnancy and delivery, help her find a Christian doula who understands and supports her adoption decision.

- Connect her to a retreat ministry that will allow her to hang out with other birth moms. Check out BirthMother Bridges in Texas. If an application is accepted, they fly in birth moms for free to attend their retreats.

- Help her talk through a decision for open or closed adoption. The adoption agency she chooses can help her work through options to find the best fit for her.

- Go along for her doctor appointments. It's hard to be alone, especially if you have to answer questions about placing for adoption from a medical team that may not fully understand that decision. Having an advocate with her helps a birth mom feel more confident as she shares her plans for the pregnancy and birth.

- If she finds a family to adopt her baby on her own and doesn't need to go through an adoption agency, she will still need an attorney. Choose a law firm that shares the goal of helping achieve the birth mother's desires for the placement. My favorite is TruAdopt Law, amazing attorney advocates for birth moms.

- BraveLove hosts birth mom dinners around the nation for her to connect and meet other birth moms while having a great time. Have her check their website to find a dinner near her.

- If a birth mom lost her child through CPS, help her, as much as you're able, as she sets out to correct the problems that caused her to lose her child to the system. If it's drugs, help her get connected to a rehab program. If there's a domestic abuse situation, encourage her to separate from her abuser and help get her back on her feet and in a safe place. If neglect was involved, help her get connected to a counselor and parenting classes. Of course, this birth mom has to *want* to help herself. As a mentor or friend, you can spin your wheels trying to get her to want to leave or change, but she ultimately has to have the desire and make the decision for herself. As she is ready for change, help her get back on her feet. Hang in there as she gets emotionally healthy and able to provide a safe environment. Then you can work together to get her kids back home.

For Supporting Foster Families and Children

- What unique gift or strength do you have that might help a foster family? There is something you can do! If you're not sure, ask God to show you. Foster families who receive emotional and physical help are more likely to continue fostering.

- Pray about becoming a foster family yourselves. There are many kids in the system who need forever families. Get more information and have your questions answered through support groups, free downloads, and awesome organizations that offer help. Check out Promise686 and LifeLine Ministries to find the right fit for you.

- If you provide a service, product, or a meal as your business, pray about offering a regular discount to foster families. These families are changing the world by opening their homes to foster children, so finding ways to help them save time or money makes a big difference. Help them save more to save more!

- Provide respite care for a foster family, occasionally babysitting or serving as an emergency contact when a need arises. You may have to be licensed by the state to offer short- or long-term care. Check with your state about how to sign up.

- Bring a foster family a meal occasionally to alleviate some of their workday stress and hustle.

- Offer to come alongside after school to help with homework and reading. Foster families with many kids at many ages could use more hands on deck to help cover school work in the afternoons and evenings.

- Donate to foster families that receive children without much time to prepare or make purchases. Gather items needed for a foster family so needs can be covered within just a few days. There is power in posting on social media. People want to help!

- Volunteer as a CASA Advocate (Court Appointed Special Advocate) by becoming authorized by the court to speak on behalf of a child in foster care. By becoming an advocate, you would spend time with the child and gather information, then take what you have learned to the judge and make a recommendation on behalf of the child.

- Churches, consider offering trauma training for foster families. There are many complexities with taking in children who have experienced mental and physical abuse. Foster families need the support of the church to navigate the blending of the families God has given them. Whether the family fosters children for a short season or forever, the church has the opportunity to support and resource the families throughout the process. Lifeline and Promise686 are amazing organizations that provide comprehensive help and support for your congregations.

- Organize a meal train for a family that has just received foster children. Receiving new children can make life chaotic at first; having meals covered gives the whole family more time to focus on the most important needs while parents and children bond with each other.

- Invite the whole family over to your house for dinner or a play date!

- Pray about being a shepherding family for a girl who has aged out of foster care. Many times she is left without a phone or any family to call if she did have one! You might let her live with you while she gets on her feet, or if she already has a place to stay just be there for her through thick and thin. Check out Unfaulted to see how to get involved!

- Make a dream come true for a male or female foster child who has aged out of the system. Donate to the Dream Makers Project with America's Kids Belong to help get a foster adult on the right path. Helping him or her get on track for success can possibly help prevent unplanned pregnancies in the future.

- Just listen. Fostering children can feel isolating at times. Stay consistent with checking with your friends to see how they are doing. Laugh with them. Cry with them. Pray with them. Don't try to fix all their problems; just listen.

National Organizations to Serve and Support

America's Kids Belong	americaskidsbelong.org
Dream Makers Project	dreammakersproject.org
BirthMother Bridge Ministries	birthmotherbridgeministries.com
BraveLove	bravelove.org
National CASA/GAL Association for Children	casagal.org
Catholic Charities	catholiccharitiesusa.org/find-help
LifeLine Children's Services	lifelinechild.org
Promise686	promise686.org
TruAdopt Law	truadopt.org
Unfaulted	unfaulted.org

FREE HER

Breaking Your Chains
So Others Can Break Theirs

There were ten thousand women in attendance at the Pink Impact conference where I was speaking. A women's ministry leader interviewed me on stage, asking questions about the history of Embrace Grace and how God had given me the idea for it at a Pink Impact conference some years earlier.

Much of what I said that day focused on how women who choose life are brave. That courage benefits the world because brave moms raise brave kids. We were wrapping up the interview, and Debbie was thanking me for being a guest when the Lord prompted me to say one more thing.

I said, "Debbie, there are ten thousand women in this arena, which means about 2,500 of you have experienced an abortion. . . . The Lord wants to start the healing process in your heart this weekend at this ministry event. Many of you feel disqualified from ministry, but God wants you to know that *He* qualifies you. You are an overcomer, and we overcome through Jesus and by sharing our stories. Your story can help save lives! He loves you so much. Just open your heart to Him."

We had two Embrace Grace vendor booths at this arena, one on each end. As I closed the interview from the stage, our team quickly made their way back to our booths because they had a sense of what God was about to do.

Then the session released, and women began flooding our booths. Many were inspired by the ministry and wanted to see how they could get involved and start a group at their own church. But what I could not get over were the hundreds of women with mascara smeared around their eyes because they had been crying so hard. Each of them looked into my eyes with *that look*, and I just knew. They didn't have to say a word.

I knew they had experienced an abortion.

Some just looked at our materials and took it all in. Others opened up about what had happened years before. And every story we heard had a common element: Fear had been the reason they had chosen abortion.

There is one woman I will never forget. She and her two sisters were wearing matching hot pink t-shirts they'd made for the conference, expecting a light-hearted, energetic weekend together. But God had different plans. More than fun, He had wanted her to be free.

She had been so moved by my message that her sisters almost had to hold her up as she walked to the booth. When they approached, one of them said quietly, "Our sister was very touched by what you said today. She asked us to bring her to meet you.

She's really emotional and having a hard time talking."

It was a long time before she could say what she wanted to say. Finally, she looked up at me with a tear-drenched face and forced out a whisper with intensity. She asked, "Do you mean to tell me that God can use *me*?"

The thought had never crossed her mind. The pain, grief, and regret of her abortion decision had fueled feelings of unworthiness. But that day something changed

God has a way of using messy people to change the world.

inside of her. Hope was rising, and she began to dream about the possibility of making a difference in the world, despite the pain from her past.

WHAT THE BIBLE HAS TO SAY
ABOUT BREAKING CHAINS

Many men and women feel as if an abortion is an unpardonable sin. They think they can never be used by God because of decisions they made in their past. They worry they have made a permanent mess of their lives. But God has a way of using messy people to change the world.

In 2 Corinthians 12:9, Paul writes about how God used his own messy life: "But he said to me, 'My grace is sufficient for you, for my power is made perfect in weakness.' Therefore I will boast all the more gladly about my weaknesses, so that Christ's power may rest on me." Our weaknesses do not disqualify us from grace. Our weaknesses display His grace.

I was recently on a pro-life radio show, and on air the host read a listener letter about a show he had done on the topic of abortion.

> Hello. I listened to yesterday's radio show. I honestly don't think there's any hope for me. I've been saved, but it's not enough. I'm struggling. Are there any counselors you can recommend? I'm afraid if I talk to someone I know, I'll be judged. I have a horrible past. I can't understand how I was able to do the things I've done. I'm a good person and have always cared about others and tried to live like Jesus . . . but when we are young, our judgment is off. I was inexperienced in life and very naive. My decisions have affected me in a way where I get physically sick. All I can think about is when my time is up, where am I really going? There is no forgiveness for murderers, and there is no way out of this! I'm so scared.

When I heard this, I wept. There are so many men and women who feel this way, and most do not have the courage to speak about it. It breaks my heart that they don't know the freedom of receiving Christ's righteousness as their own. They don't know that God can bring beauty and healing from the pain of wrong decisions. There is no sin God can't forgive—including abortion. Whether you encouraged and paid for your girlfriend to have an abortion, or if you had an abortion yourself, God will forgive. His mercy, forgiveness, and grace apply to the sin of abortion just as it does to every other sin.

Our weaknesses do not disqualify us from grace. Our weaknesses display His grace.

No matter what we've done or who we are, God loves us so much. He promises to forgive us, totally and completely, if we will only turn to Him in repentance and faith. The Bible says, "If we confess our sins, he is faithful and just and will forgive us our sins and purify us from all unrighteousness" (1 John 1:9). All we have to do to receive forgiveness is confess, admitting we need Him.

Freedom is only a prayer away.

If you are reading this and have experienced an abortion, please open your heart to God. He wants to relieve your heartbreak and heal you. The lingering ache of having an abortion isn't something you will simply get over, but God can show you how to drop the chains of pain. Freedom is what He's all about.

Christine Caine talked about freedom and moving forward in a *Relevant Magazine* interview:

> It's getting up every day knowing that Christ in me is the hope of glory and that I can do what God has called me to do for that day. I think I was so riddled by shame for so much of my life that I never thought I could do what God called me to do. . . . Today I can put one foot in front of the other and hold my head up high and go where I feel the Spirit of God is calling me. I think that is what walking shame-free is. It's that I'm not going to allow my own limitations or what people have said to me or what people have done to me define where I'm going. In other words, I think most people go into the future, but they are just totally stuck in their past. They've allowed their history to define their destiny. Once you decide you're going to drop your baggage and deal with your stuff, you can step into

your destiny for the first time in your life—and you are just not living an eternal yesterday.[1]

Confession is the key. Part of our healing involves telling someone. What you bring out into the light has no power over you anymore. What you keep in the darkness is what Satan will use to torment you.

Revelation 12:11 says, "They triumphed over him by the blood of the Lamb and by the word of their testimony." Some translations say, "They overcame him . . ." When we share our stories, that is how we overcome. When we open our hearts by opening our mouths, it gives other people the courage to share their stories too.

Sometimes women and men come up to me after I speak at events and lean in really close to whisper their abortion story. I'm so glad that they felt I would honor their vulnerability. I am proud of anyone who takes that tentative first step to share. Every time we offer the sacrifice of our stories, God is glorified, and our voice gets a little louder and more confident.

DISCOVERING YOUR PLACE

Many churches speak about life and abortion once every January for Sanctity of Life month. And pastors wonder if mentioning the sanctity of life only once a year is often enough. While we don't need weekly sermons about how abortion is wrong, we do need almost constant reminders that there is hope and healing from the sins of the past, including healing after abortion. Those who are hurting and struggling with shame or deep regret need to hear that message of hope spoken out loud. Somewhere, sometime, church leaders need to say out loud that the church is a safe place to talk it through if someone is considering an abortion.

Abby Johnson used to be the Director of a Planned Parenthood abortion clinic. Now she is a pro-life advocate and the author of *Unplanned: The Dramatic True Story of a Former Planned Parenthood Leader's Eye-Opening Journey across the Life Line.* Once, a pastor asked Abby, "Am I doing enough by talking about it once a year?"

She responded passionately: "I don't know, but I will say that when I worked at Planned Parenthood, it was not uncommon for a woman to be holding a rosary or Bible in her hands while she laid on the abortion table. So you tell me, how often should you preach about abortion?"[2]

Pastors know their congregations and should consider how, when, and where it's best to bring up abortion and healing after abortion with their church communities. But this much is sure: the more often church leaders talk about abortion, the more the people with questions about abortion will talk about it, too. Where will they turn? Who should they ask? If they know the church culture welcomes the opportunity to talk it through, there's a better chance they'll bring it up to church folks. We have seen that personal relationships are what it takes to turn the tide of abortion, and churches can exercise leadership in fostering vulnerable relationships.

We *need* you to serve in the pro-life movement, especially if you have some connection to or experience with abortion.

Perhaps your own mother has let you know that she considered abortion. Maybe you have been the one who was on the abortion table at one critical time in your life. Some of you chose to go through with it. Some of you didn't. Nothing disqualifies you from the call to help. If you have been touched by abortion, then we need you, we need you, we need you.

A word of caution: If you've experienced an abortion, prayerfully consider going through an abortion healing program before you start serving in the pro-life movement. It's not a prerequisite, of course, but sometimes a short (eight to twelve weeks) healing class or group can make a world of difference.

I know it's not easy to open up in such a tender way, but sometimes discovering you are not alone accelerates the healing process. Abortion healing programs are offered at churches and pregnancy centers all over the nation, with varied options to try. If you prefer one-on-one help, you might sign up for a mentor. Or you can choose a small support group that works through a curriculum together. There are also weekend intensive retreats that offer a deep-dive into freedom and healing.

Be what *you* needed.

WHAT FREEING HER CAN LOOK LIKE

If you have had an abortion, think about what you really needed at the time of your decision. What would have given you the courage to choose life? You can fill the void for someone else and show up for them the way you wish someone had shown up for you.

Be what *you* needed.

Gabrielle has learned to do just that. She says,

> Serving in the pro-life movement has helped me realize
> that sharing my abortion story, which I thought I would
> never share because of shame and guilt, could not only
> save one person but *two*: the mommy and baby. I may
> have lost one baby, but I'm ready to help save thousands.
> I can only thank God for using my pastor to show God's
> amazing love and forgiveness, because without those two
> things I would not be able to say any of this. God has led
> me to serve single and pregnant women to not only heal
> myself from my past but to help others not to have to go
> through what I did because of my abortion.

God can work through you and your story. You might serve at
a pregnancy center and use your gifts to bring hope and comfort
to a young woman with an unplanned pregnancy. Lead an Embrace Grace group and disciple and love her into the arms of Jesus.
Lead an abortion healing group at your church or pregnancy
center. Create a safe place for women who have experienced an
abortion to help them grieve and heal, then activate them to get
involved in the pro-life movement themselves.

You can do anything. Just do something.

And Then There Were None is an organization that frees
abortion workers to leave the abortion industry, covering expenses during the transition and helping them find new jobs in
the medical field. Their goal is to end abortion from the inside
out. They offer healing retreats for the workers, loving them
through the process and beyond.

And Then There Were None needs volunteers. They need people to help former abortion workers look for job opportunities, help them with resume writing, and find other resources to assist with the transition.

Using your story to serve, heal, and help will not only change the lives of others, it will change yours, too.

I received the following letter from one of our Embrace Grace leaders. She and her husband are pastors at their church, and she had always hidden her past experience with abortion because she feared it would bring condemnation. As a result, she had never completely healed.

> A young lady from our campus gave me some flyers and asked that I review and approve them to be displayed in the areas I oversaw. I read the top portion, and it said *Embrace Grace*. As I read the rest of the flyer, I felt an immediate sense of anxiety overtake me. I looked up from the paper and felt as if the entire lobby stopped what they were doing and were all staring at me as I read the flyer. It was scary! I shrank into my fear and put the flyers aside.
>
> Later as my husband and I were talking during lunch, I told him how I felt when I read the flyer. And then I said, "Remember how I shared God was speaking to me about being authentic and walking authentically as I lead? . . . I get it now! I know exactly why He is calling me to a higher level of authenticity. I know what He wants me to do!"
>
> My husband was 100 percent supportive, of course. (I'm blessed!) The fact that I was so scared to be involved in a group where I would be sharing my story was

exactly why I knew this is where God wanted me. Living authentically does not leave room for fear. I wasn't leading to the full potential He called me to. How can I lead others when I was still chained to shame, guilt, fear, and condemnation? So I needed to face fear and trade it for living freely. He has called me to be *free*.

Later that week I contacted the young lady taking charge in starting an Embrace Grace group at our church and asked to meet with her. She was the first person other than my husband and parents who I'd shared my past with. It was terrifying and freeing at the same time! After sharing my story, I shared how God was working on me over the past few years and preparing me for this moment. I expressed my interest in becoming part of her team (still shaking in my boots). She graciously allowed me to come into that first semester, observe, and share when I felt ready to do so.

I am so grateful she allowed me to be a part. The first semester was a time for me to sit back and allow Embrace Grace to continue healing my heart. What I previously viewed as a stumbling block ended up being God's purpose and calling in my life. (I cry tears of gratitude as I type this because I would have NEVER imagined God would use all my junk to bless others.)

As our next semester started, I began sharing the teaching role with the other leaders and really bonded with the single and pregnant moms. I just love being able to love on them! Embrace Grace is part of who I am, and I cannot see advancing the Kingdom hand in hand with other church leaders without this calling of Embrace

Grace. God is moving in this ministry, and women are being freed from their chains and authentically walking in their calling to bless and encourage the younger generation. Our church culture has always been inviting, and we even use the slogan "No perfect people allowed," which has been freeing for other women who are leaders in the church to share their past story of abortion, adoption, and being a young mother.

Thank you for helping me be brave!

Whether you've had an abortion yourself or your heart just breaks for those who have, follow the map of your heartbreak and partner with heaven to heal others. Guilt and shame have no hold on you; they have no power to hold you back from your role in the Kingdom.

One life may have been lost to abortion, but it doesn't have to be two.

Ideas for How to Free Her

- Start an abortion healing support group at your church. Check out Surrendering the Secret curriculum through Lifeway, or research and find an abortion healing book or curriculum you love and connect with.

- Help another woman tell her story even if it's with just one person. We overcome by sharing our testimonies and through the blood of the Lamb. Even if it starts with just writing it down in a note and saving it for later or giving her courage to share with just one other person, it gets a little easier every time she shares it. It's also possible to share a story anonymously online at AbortionChangesYou.com.

- Help her get started on her healing. Support After Abortion is an organization that will help her find whatever kind of healing she is ready for. If she wants a healing resource to do on her own at her own pace, or if she wants a mentor, small group at a church or pregnancy center, or a healing retreat, Support After Abortion can help her find the support and healing she needs, wherever she lives.

- Would she rather just get out of town with other women and take a deep dive into allowing God to begin healing her heart from abortion? Rachel's Vineyard offers a great abortion healing retreat that happens through Catholic churches all over the nation.

- Help her get connected to a pro-life ministry where she can serve. Helping women with unplanned pregnancies and being the person she wishes she'd had in her life when she made her abortion decision can help her heal by serving others.

- Honor her baby's life that was lost by helping her memorialize her baby with a plaque with the baby's name on it, with a piece of jewelry with her baby's initial, by releasing balloons containing a letter to the baby, or by making a donation to a pregnancy center in the baby's honor.

- Give her a journal so she can start to write out her thoughts, feelings, and emotions connected to her abortion. As she digs deep and pours out her heart on paper, God will reveal His heart of love and forgiveness toward her.

- Just listen. Allow her to express her emotions as she shares her story with you. She may be feeling anger, sadness, grief, shame, and heartbreak. Be a safe place for her to vent as she processes it all, and remind her of how God sees her and loves her.

- Help her research symptoms of Abortion PTSD. If she relates to three or more symptoms, an abortion recovery class or support group or professional counseling could help.

- Connect her with a counselor by phone at Focus on the Family. They offer a one-time complimentary consultation from a Christian perspective. They also provide referrals for licensed Christian counselors in your area.

National Organizations to Serve and Support

Abortion Changes You	abortionchangesyou.com
Focus on the Family	focusonthefamily.com/Get-Help/Counseling-Services-and-Referrals/
Her Choice to Heal	herchoicetoheal.com
Support After Abortion	supportafterabortion.com
Surrendering the Secret	surrenderingthesecret.com

8

EMPOWER HER

Ending the Cycle of Poverty

I once delivered baby formula to a homeless mom. One of the moms in our Embrace Grace group had told us her friend Hannah needed help. I called beforehand to see what else she needed. The matter-of-fact way she approached our conversation broke my heart. She had come to accept her poverty as a normal way of life.

> **Me**: Hi, Brittney gave me your name and number. She said that you ran out of baby formula for your baby. Is that true?
>
> **Hannah**: Yes, ma'am. I ran out this morning. There's no money left on my WIC card, and I don't have any income coming in 'til the first of the month. I'm just really in a bad spot.
>
> **Me**: Are you at a hotel?

Hannah: No, I was. But I used all the money I had to live there for a while, and now I don't have a place to go. I can sleep on this guy's couch for a few nights, but he said I have to leave after this. It's not really a safe place for me and the baby. But it's the only place I have to go.

Me: Do you have food for yourself? How are you eating?

Hannah: I'm okay. I don't need food. I stole some this morning.

Me: You stole some? Okay, what about diapers? Do you need those?

Hannah: No, ma'am. I stole diapers, as well. I'm okay with that. I just need formula. It's hard to steal formula because of the sensors they put on the cans. She hasn't eaten since this morning so I know she's hungry.

Me: Oh, my goodness. Okay, send me your address. I'll stop by.

By the time I had a chance to gather things for Hannah, it was late so my husband decided to go with me. She was staying in a part of town known for crime. We brought food, diapers, and a grocery store gift card. Hannah came out on the porch, and I got a chance to talk with her a bit more. She told me she was only going to stay on this man's couch for a few days. Then she would have to figure out where to go next.

Me: Isn't there anywhere else you can go? Do you have a mom? Can you live with her?

Hannah: That's where I just came from. My mom is addicted to cocaine. It's gotten really bad, and it's not safe for me and the baby. I left my twin sisters there. They are seventeen years old. I worry so much about them. I wish they were with me.

Me: What about your dad? Can you live with your dad?

Hannah: I have never had a relationship with my dad. He has twenty-one kids. He lives in a small mobile home, and he has very young children. I would just be in the way if I were there. There is not enough room for everyone as it is.

Me: Oh. Can I stop and pray for you right now?

I prayed for her, and she cried. Keeping it full of hope, I prayed for God to answer her prayers and do a miracle in her life. But even as I said the words, in my heart I felt this might be a hopeless situation. She didn't just need food and diapers. She needed *everything*. Where would we even start?

> **Me**: Is your baby okay? I know she hasn't eaten since this morning. I can't imagine how fussy and hungry she is. Is she crying a lot?
>
> **Hannah**: No, not really. She's just whimpering a little.

As I left, I couldn't get those last words out of my head. "Not really . . . she's just whimpering a little." I thought about how when my children were babies, I would try my best to make it three or four hours between feeding times, but my kids always *screamed* for milk before it was time. It had been close to eleven hours since Hannah's baby had eaten. How could she just be . . . *whimpering*?

As soon as I had the thought, God started showing me the difference. My babies cried because they knew I would meet their needs. If they cried for milk, I gave them milk. But this sweet baby already knew that when she cries for milk, most likely it's not coming. So why cry? At just five months old, she had already learned there is no point trying to get what she wants or needs because nothing is coming.

I couldn't stop crying. A baby already believing there is nothing out there for her? These babies grow up to be kids who can't see the point of trying at school if there's nothing out there for them. Those kids grow up to be adults who deeply believe there is no point in pursuing their dreams, because nothing is coming.

God can multiply our simple efforts for a big impact.

And so the cycle continues, generation after generation.

More than 30 percent of single moms live below the poverty line,[1] which is an annual income of $12,490.[2] And the government makes it hard to get off the welfare system. As soon as a welfare recipient crosses an income threshold, even by a *little* bit, assistance stops altogether—before they are making enough to support their families. Unless there's a ladder from government dependency to full financial independence, they can almost never break out. We have an awesome opportunity as a church to be that ladder. We can help break generational patterns and help single moms work toward their dreams.

God can multiply our simple efforts for a big impact. Even in a life like Hannah's, which seems so hopeless from a human perspective, God will provide in miraculous ways.

We posted about Hannah on social media and listed *all* the things she needed: a two-bedroom apartment (so there was enough room for her and her twin sisters), beds with comforters, cleaning supplies, baby nursery items, food, a job, and a car. Who would provide all of that? Even while we were posting her needs on social media, we had our doubts.

Oh, the Lord knew what He was doing when He created the church!

Get ready for this.

In *one* week, every single need was met—even the car.

Hannah's story isn't over. She got a job as a janitor at a local church, with a flexible schedule so she could register for school. God can change the most hopeless situation and turn it around quickly. What seemed too big to even ask God for, He accomplished in record time. We were praying on that dark and lonely porch on a Saturday night. By the *next* Saturday night, the body of Christ was helping Hannah move into her own apartment.

Transformation is what Embrace Grace is all about, and we see God transforming lives, again and again, one young woman at a time.

WHAT THE BIBLE HAS TO SAY
ABOUT POVERTY

Hagar is the first single mom mentioned in the Bible. Her story is recorded in Genesis 16 and 21. Hagar is a slave belonging to Sarah, the wife of Abraham. It is Sarah's task to produce a son and heir for her husband, but when she cannot, she gives Hagar to her husband as a surrogate. Hagar becomes pregnant, and God promises that her child will be the founder of a great nation. She gives birth to a son, Ishmael.

Sarah grows to despise Hagar and treats her terribly. Hagar has no one to fight for her so she packs up the few belongings she has, takes her son, and flees to the desert to escape the torment. Hagar is in survival mode.

God cares deeply for single moms. He wants to provide for their needs— and He does that through the church.

At one point in her journey, she runs out of resources. She is homeless and without food or water, feeling defeated and devastated. She places her thirsty and dehydrated son under a bit of shade and turns away. She doesn't want him to see her cry, and she doesn't want to see him die.

Ishmael, Hagar's son, begins to whimper and cry.

> God heard the boy crying, and the angel of God called to Hagar from heaven and said to her, "What is the matter, Hagar? Do not be afraid; God has heard the boy crying as he lies there. Lift the boy up and take him by the hand, for I will make him into a great nation."
>
> Then God opened her eyes and she saw a well of water. So she went and filled the skin with water and gave the boy a drink (Gen. 21:17–19).

After receiving His miraculous provision, Hagar begins to refer to God in a new way. She gives "this name to the LORD who spoke to her: 'You are the God who sees me,' for she said, 'I have now seen the One who sees me'" (Gen. 16:13). This precious single mother orients her understanding of life around God's character. Even her son Ishmael, the first child raised by a single parent in the Bible, has a name that means "God Hears."

Just like Hagar, single moms can find themselves rejected and alone. Their goal is to provide the best for their kids even when it's hard. God cares deeply for single moms. He sees them and hears their children's cries. He wants to provide for their needs.

And He does that through the church.

DISCOVERING YOUR PLACE

When a single mom or dad invites God into their parenting, He empowers them. He equips them with everything they need to be that child's parent. It is a simple equation, really: One Parent + God = Success.

Experiencing an unplanned pregnancy can be completely overwhelming to a single mom. It isn't easy to figure out daycare, find and keep a job that will provide enough, establish co-parenting routines with the father of the baby (if he's involved), and much more.

She does all of this . . . alone.

If a single mom already has kids and is pregnant again, she might feel like throwing up her hands in total despair. The abortion rate is higher when a woman is pregnant again after already having one or more children.[3] These moms feel their lives are over.

When working with single parents, the challenge feels big,

beyond the human imagination. There are so many issues and needs. It takes a tender heart and a sensitive spirit to discern what to do. Sometimes God wants us to help, but sometimes He wants us to get out of the way and watch Him do it. Every circumstance is different, and yet they have one thing in common: they need us to be there, cheering them on and looking out for them. We can believe in single moms and call out greatness in them.

Remember, it was not the person you believed in the most who made the biggest difference in your life, but it was the person who believed in and supported you.

No one wants to receive help that feels like a *handout*, given out of a sense of duty. But almost anyone will receive a *hand up*, which feels like empowerment. This physical blessing is every bit as important as a spiritual blessing. In fact, it *is* a spiritual blessing. Providing for the simple daily needs of single parents and their children is not just about the here and now; it is a matter of eternal significance.

People have a really hard time hearing the good news about Jesus if their stomachs are empty.

WHAT EMPOWERING HER CAN LOOK LIKE

Taylor had signed up to attend an Embrace Grace class but had unexpectedly gone into labor early. She was unprepared and had nothing for the baby. When she reached out for help, we posted on social media to see if anyone wanted to cover necessities for her, specifically a car seat. A group of women came forward to meet the need. Two hours after Taylor gave birth, our team texted her to let her know a crib and car seat were on the way. She immediately began thanking Jesus. She accepted Jesus as her Savior right there in the hospital bed! The same day she received the gift of a child in her arms, she received the gift of eternal life from her heavenly Father.

Best day ever!

There are so many creative and practical ways you can help a single mom. One of our moms said that just helping take out the trash was a huge help:

> I was a single momma, and living alone was hard with a newborn. I had a little one-bedroom apartment in the "hood," and when my trash got full I would put the bag outside my door. Just carrying trash to the dumpster took work! Many times I would walk out, and it would already be gone and thrown in the dumpster for me! That was five years ago, but I will always remember that—how Jesus took that trash out for me. Larissa W.

Another small act of kindness connected this single mom to a church family:

> I was at QuikTrip thirteen years ago, getting my daughter and me muffins for breakfast because I had no money for real food. I was putting my last $20 in the gas tank to look for a job. A man told the clerk to buy all my stuff and my gas with his card and told me that God wanted him to do it and that he was a part of Gateway Church. Two years later, I looked into Gateway and found my spiritual family because of him. Carina T.

One church's love bomb was given to a mom the very first time she attended church. This act of kindness inspired her eventually to start leading an Embrace Grace group. By now, she has helped hundreds of single moms:

> One year for Mother's Day my neighbor invited me to their church because they were having an event for single moms. We had a nice lunch, and they had door prizes. I won the grand prize, and it was a room makeover. Volunteers came to my house and decorated a room of my choosing and in my taste. They made my daughter a sweet little dressing table with a mirror. It was so cute and so thoughtful. I felt loved … without any agenda … just loved. I told them I intended to pay their kindness forward. It was the first (and only) time anyone invited me and my baby to church. Beth P.

An Embrace Grace leader's church easily stepped in and helped in this unique way:

> We have an Embrace Grace mom from last semester who goes to our church. She was in need of two new tires (having to fill up a tire daily). I mentioned it to our pastor's wife and asked if anyone in the church dealt with tires. I wanted to help her get tires but knew I couldn't afford them so I was hoping to get a discount and try to help cover the cost. Our pastor mentioned it at the business meeting last night, and people gave an offering to buy her four brand new tires! Isn't God good? She

never asked for help, and that was way beyond what I was looking for. Embrace Grace Leader

God may be calling you to give a financial gift that is big and extravagant, and maybe He is urging you to invite a single mom into your home for a safe place to live for a while. God might be asking you to partner with a local maternity home. They are places that allow a single and pregnant mom time to catch her breath, receive healing, make a game plan for income, and work on job security.

Your offer of help doesn't have to be elaborate. Sometimes, the best thing you can do is bring the mom a meal, hold the baby, and love them both.

Samantha has used her passion for baking to provide emergency housing for single moms. She started a company called She Rises Gluten Free Cookie Company, and the story behind the "why" is beautiful:

> I saw a single mother of five children at the play area at church, and as soon as I saw her, I could tell something was wrong. I asked if she was okay, and she responded by sharing that she and her five children were living in an extended-stay hotel and she only had enough money to pay for two more weeks. She was currently looking for a job but hadn't found one yet. Her trailer home had caught on fire in July of that year and at six months pregnant with her fifth child, they became homeless overnight. Shortly after the fire she lost her job from the ensuing depression and hopelessness. She said, "I kept trying to pull it together, but all I could do was cry."

Samantha couldn't just walk away from Angie and her children. She spent the next two weeks frantically making phone calls, trying to find a shelter that would accept another family, but homeless shelters often have regulations on how many children they can accept, and five in one family was too many. Shelter after shelter turned Angie away. They just didn't have enough beds.

At the time, Samantha worked in single parent ministry, so she had access to more resources than most. Working with the nonprofit organizations she knew, she checked on every available option for transitional housing, but there was always something that closed the door—and kept Angie locked out.

Samantha pulled together her personal savings but could only commit to providing one more week of rent at the extended-stay hotel. And then what?

When she didn't know what else to do, Samantha turned to Facebook. She made one impassioned plea for help. That was all it took. Her friends read the single mother's story and rallied like champions, offering funds that would allow them to make a legitimate plan to help this family transition into permanent housing.

Samantha can hardly believe the way the Lord has turned this story around for Angie and for her:

> Today, [Angie] is doing amazing. She stops by my office about every six weeks to give me an update. At our last meeting, she told me she can finally look people in the eye, where before, she had so much shame she couldn't make eye contact with anyone. She is employed, and she has hope. She told me that for the first time in her life, she truly believes that God loves her. Her life was forever

changed by the love of people who did not even know her but wanted to help her. They were the hands and feet of Jesus....

Working in Single Parent Ministry for eleven years, I know firsthand how the system works against you.... There is a gap from government dependency to self-sufficiency.

I personally believe the church is to be that ladder that bridges the gap, and when I say "church" I am not talking about an organization, I am talking about people. People make up the church, not the building. The hand of government can never do what the heart of God can. But I knew I could not keep going to Facebook to ask for money or to my friends. So I asked the Lord for a way to make money, and this is where She Rises Gluten Free Cookie Company was birthed.

She Rises Cookie Company hires single moms to make, package, and deliver the cookies, and a portion of the company profits go to helping women and children like Angie. Amazing, isn't it?! Samantha is using her passion and gifts to make a difference in her community.

What is *your* passion?

If you are enthusiastic about education, there are so many ways you can teach. You can help a single mom get her GED. Maybe she doesn't know where to start and needs extra tutoring in order to pass. Or maybe she needs someone to babysit her child a few hours a week so she can have focused study time.

Gateway Church even has a Single Parent Family Night once a week at one of their campuses. Most of the parents are coming straight from work and daycare, and they don't have time to go home and cook a meal or the extra funds to pick up food on the way. The church provides a free dinner for the parent and his or her children. After the meal, the parent can go into a Bible study with other single parents while their children go into children's church, but they also offer free tutoring for kids of single parents. Volunteers who love to teach and mentor will sit with a child and help with homework or tutoring in an area of struggle at school. They pray with the children and show them they are loved. It's such a relief for the single parents to know they can focus on being filled with God's Word while their children are cared for and well fed.

Giving is a joy when you match your offering to your passion.

Sheila is a volunteer who loves to help single moms find great scholarships. Then she mentors the moms all through their college years as a support system and cheerleader. She has a heart to keep motivating and encouraging when a single mom might want to give up and quit.

Danny is delighted to educate single moms on money management, teaching them how they can make wise financial decisions even on little income.

Trent enjoys giving extravagantly to a junior college that provides childcare on premises for single moms. He wants student parents to know that they can have their babies and their dreams of graduating, too.

Have you heard the term *random acts of kindness*? It usually refers to small gestures designed to make someone's day. But in Embrace Grace, sometimes those words just don't go far enough.

I have started using the term *love bomb* to describe an enormous gift or blessing given to a single and pregnant momma. These are much more than "acts of kindness." They are "kindness explosions."

One of my favorite love bombs was a car for a single mom. She didn't have any family and was moving to a new town to get away from bad influences back home. She wanted a fresh start now that she was pregnant with a son. She had found an apartment but didn't have a bed or furnishings so she was sleeping on the floor. We did a quick Facebook post, and within hours, people had committed to give her everything she needed.

But the best gift was a car.

This single mom had no car and would walk or Uber to work. One man who saw our post knew he was supposed to give her the car he was about to sell because he had just purchased a new one for his wife.

He left this note in the car for her:

> *Valerie,*
>
> *Although we don't know you, we definitely have something in common now. Over the past ten years, this car—"Beauty"—has been such a great car. We brought our first boy home just after getting the car, and then our second son a few years later. We've driven all over on trips, vacations, and family reunions in Beauty. This car was our first purchase after financial hard times. This car means a lot to us. Now we hope and pray that Beauty continues to be a wonderful car for you! When we heard about you, our hearts leapt, knowing you were the one for Beauty. So just know that today you are*

loved, not only by God our Father and Embrace Grace, but also by a family praying for you and cheering you on to be the best mom ever.

Things to know about Beauty:

1. *She runs perfectly.*
2. *We change the oil every 3,000 miles, and you should too! You need to take it to General Auto for the oil change really soon. It's already paid for; just tell them you need an oil change and give them my name. I was going to change it but ran out of time.*
3. *The remote broke, and I bought a new remote cover. The red panic button is really the trunk opener.*
4. *The trunk opener switch is under the driver door handle.*
5. *The gas has to be opened by a lever on the driver floorboard.*
6. *Beauty has a pretty new battery.*
7. *The red key is a valet key.*
8. *I left a guide in the cup holder to help, along with the wheel lock key. Leave this in the glove box because you can't remove the wheels without it.*
9. *We left one CD for you titled "You Are Loved."*

Isn't that sweet? It's like a daddy's note for his daughter. Even though this man never met Valerie, he felt compelled to give in this way. This car was up there in age (hence, the CD player), but she didn't care. She was *thrilled* to have a car that ran perfectly! Valerie accepted Christ as her Savior the very next week, just a few days before she gave birth to the most handsome little boy.

Rarely is it just *one* thing that made the difference; it was a community of people who acted when the Lord spoke. It was a community being the hands and feet of Jesus. Whether they donated a cooking pan, picked up and delivered furniture, spoke life when a mom felt the most broken, gave her an extra tip as she waited on their table, put a Bible on her doorstep, or bought her a car, those acts added up to a life transformed. When we stay obedient to what God asks of us and open our eyes to people around us who crave hope, we start seeing change in our local communities, our states, and the world.

We can have open hands and open hearts to give in a way the Lord asks of us. When we share this way, our *own* lives are changed.

No love bomb is the same. They come big, and they come small, but all of them empower single mothers to step out of the cycle of poverty. When people leave their comfort zones to do something nice for someone, it allows the recipient a glimpse of hope for her life.

God knows that when His people drop a love bomb on someone in need, it often catches their hearts on fire for Him.

Ideas for How to Empower Her

- Start a Facebook private group to empower the single moms in your circle to help each other and encourage each other. Single moms helping single moms is beautiful! We are sisters in Christ.

- Listen. Be a sounding board. Be a friend. Single parents don't have a spouse to talk things through with, so having a friend who is consistently there to listen and lean on is helpful.

- Babysit her kids regularly. Make it a weekly or monthly treat for her to look forward to, whether she gets a night out or just some time to catch up with chores around the house without little people under her feet.

- Create opportunities for her to tell her stories of the obstacles she has overcome. Teach her how to tell her testimony. Empower her to be bold.

- Share celebratory milestone moments with her and her kids. Celebrate birthdays, holidays, beginning of a school year, and the launch of summer. Most single moms don't have anyone to share the excitement of milestones for her kids.

- Set up a day each month to come to her house for three hours and just visit, help in the kitchen, hold a baby, or whatever she needs to refresh her soul.

- Are you great at organizing? Declutter and organize the kids' room and toys. An organized house creates a more relaxing atmosphere.

- Text her an encouragement throughout the week or mail encouraging cards when God places her on your heart.

- Support organizations like Let Them Live that help eliminate a mother's need to choose abortion due to financial burdens. Let Them Live helps them with the support pregnant moms need to successfully carry babies to term.

- Take her to the local car wash and bless her with a deep cleaning, inside and out. There is nothing like a clean car to help you feel like you can breathe a little easier.

- Cover the cost of her bus transportation or Uber bills for a month or year so she can put money aside toward purchasing a car.

- Do a makeover on her bedroom. Ask about her favorite colors and style and tell her you would love to help her create a peaceful sanctuary of rest in her home.

- Create a homemade inspirational book of your favorite Scriptures that she can access any time, or cut strips with printed Scriptures to put in a cute bowl or jar so she can randomly pull one out any time she needs encouragement.

- Visit her one night after the kids go to bed and bring a movie and popcorn. Having girl time with laughter and food is good for the soul.

- Hire someone to cut her grass or commit yourself to doing it while her baby is small.

- Are you a do-it-yourself-er? Help with home repairs, offer to hang things, or assemble a crib or other new baby items she receives.

- Gas adds up quickly. Gas cards make great random love bombs.

- Are you good at cooking? Cook a meal or help plan meals for a week. Bring meals that are easy to pop in the oven and heat.

Or if you are a frugal cook and shopper, help her budget to stretch her food dollars. Cooking with a budget is a gift that keeps on giving.

- Have a food delivery service deliver a surprise lunch! Or teach her about healthy eating. She may not know that certain foods can help with her focus and mood.

- Start a run/walk group for single moms who can bring along their kids for exercise and girl time while working on staying healthy.

- Have flowers delivered to her on Mother's Day or any day.

- When you're buying a gift card for someone else, purchase an extra one to keep on hand for a single mom who needs encouragement.

- Bring by "life" supplies—things she needs but aren't much fun to buy, such as cleaning supplies, toilet paper, or paper towels.

- Do her grocery shopping, or babysit so she can shop kid-free. That can feel like the best break ever!

- Offer a longer day of babysitting time so she can have a day of window-shopping, coffee, and a ride through town. The bonus for you? You get to cuddle the baby!

- Help connect her to other single moms. Introduce her to friends who have kids the same age. Friendship with others in similar situations will help her feel less alone.

- Give her your phone number to use as a hotline when she or her kids are sick. It's hard to go to the drugstore and take kids with you when one of them has a fever. Be on call for emergencies so you can grab what she needs when she needs it most.

- Include her kids on special and fun outings. Many single moms say they wish their kids could have more fun experiences like museums, theme parks, and movies. There usually just isn't enough money in the budget for these extras. Or consider buying a season pass for one of these places for her and her family to enjoy!

- Go with her to court if she is in a custody battle. Hold her hand. Pray over her. Encourage her and be an advocate for her.

- Compliment her children. Call out the strengths and gifts you see in them. Mention it when she's doing a great job as a mom.

- If you're an employer, offer grace when daycare calls and she has to pick up her kid because he/she is sick. Also, provide adequate maternity leave so she can bond with her baby.

- Help a single mom move. Moving is almost impossible unless she knows someone who has a truck and is strong. Hiring movers can be expensive. If you are physically unable or do not have a truck, maybe cover the cost of pizza for the friends who come to help her move (that could be an incentive for them to come help. Everybody loves free food!).

- Men and pastors, consider filling in at school events like Donuts for Dad or other "father/child" activities so the single mom doesn't have to send her child alone and feel left out.

- Do your kids go to the same school as a single mom's kids? Offer to drop off and pick up kids at school, or care for her kids after school if she's at work and you're at home. If her kids cover most of their homework at your house, she might be able to relax and focus on fun with the kids at the end of a long day.

- With your church or other organization, host a Single Parents Night Out. Offer childcare so single parents can drop their kids at the church for a fun night while they run errands or enjoy time with friends.

- Healthy couples might "adopt" a single mom and her children, if they don't have much family (or supportive family) to share in family holiday traditions and fun activities.

- Some new mothers have come out of hurtful or broken family situations. As you invite such a mom into your home, keep it real but let her in to see how healthy families, by God's grace and with His help, solve problems, resolve conflicts, and build relationships. Disciple her, even while you make her feel at home.

- Host an Auto Repair Day for single moms, or help cover the expenses of a car repair. The cost of an unexpected repair could cut into her budget for food or rent. Every little setback can feel like a big one to her.

- Cover the daycare costs for a single mom for even one week per month. This would be such a financial relief!

- Offer tutoring for her children, or help your church organize volunteer tutors to serve on your Single Parent Family Nights.

- Are you great at managing money? Help with her budgeting and financial planning. Ask about her dreams and goals, and see if there might be ways to shape her budget to help her achieve her goal. Or help her get connected to financial courses for moms on a tight budget.

- Research and document resources in your community that offer help so you'll have them handy when a single mom needs assistance.

- Research college grants for single moms, which can be hard to find. Show her where to look for them and coach her on her applications and essays.

- Find out about her dreams. Maybe help her raise funds to cover expenses for vocational or specialty school, or raise money for the basics she might need to start a small business (like a laptop or tools or a camera). You might be able to help remove some obstacle in the way of her dreams.

- Mentor and disciple regularly.

- If the father of the baby is willing, find a godly male mentor for him too (even if they are not together).

- Help with job search, resume writing, and interview clothing. Help her feel confident and prepared as she walks in to interview for her dream job.

- Start an Embrace Life group at your church! Embrace Grace has a Part 2 group for single young moms that covers Parenting, Purity, Identity, Dreams and Goals, Dating, Financial Stewardship, Time Management, Boundaries, and so much more! It is a digital curriculum so it's easy to lead. Anyone can press Play!

- Send her on a weekend vacation with her kids. She would love to make memories with them, but often a vacation seems almost impossible.

- Get a group of friends to "adopt" a single mom in your community. Everyone can use their unique skills to serve her by helping plan birthday parties, budgeting, teaching how to cook, meal plan, etc.

- Get a group of ladies who love to decorate to undertake projects as needed; room makeovers, painting, etc.

- If she needs housing, search online for free Maternity Homes or Single Parent Housing that would allow her to live there to help her get back on her feet. If there are no maternity homes in your area, consider other cities, or even other states. Some homes will cover the expense of getting a mother to them for safety and shelter.

- Offer your own home as a shepherd home for a homeless pregnant mom or a single mom. Help her catch her breath and get her pointed in the right direction to get back on her own two feet.

- Women often choose abortion because of the financial responsibility of parenting. Find out about her greatest needs and see if your church members can come together to help meet the need so she will be empowered to choose life.

- Pray *for* her and *with* her always.

National Organizations to Serve and Support

Embrace Life	embracegrace.com
Let Them Live	letthemlive.org
Pro-Love Ministries	loveline.com

KNOW HER

Paving the Way for Pure Hearts

When my daughter Mackenzie turned sixteen, she came to me and said she would like to get a "purity ring" and that she had found a style that she loved. She was even willing to spend her own money on it. When she asked me, I immediately cringed a little on the inside. For those of you who have never heard of a purity ring, it's a ring (any ring will do) that symbolizes a commitment to abstain from sex until marriage. It became super popular in the '90s with "True Love Waits" slogans on t-shirts and etched on the inside of rings. It's not so popular now, but still many young women wear them.

You might think I'm weird for getting "cringy" about the ring. I should be proud and excited that my beautiful teenage daughter wants to make such a commitment. And I am!

The issue is that I've met and mentored hundreds of young ladies, and I've seen a pattern with the women who grew up in the church, especially those who had a purity ring at one time. After one of them has had sex, she tells me she has "lost her purity." And since she's "lost her purity," she might just as well not hold back from having sex. Many girls see themselves as dirty, and with a cycle of shame, they end up with more regrets, shame, and isolation. Having lost hope of purity, this girl stuffs her purity ring into the bottom corner of her jewelry box, or worse, she throws it away. She feels sure she does not deserve God's best for a future husband so she stays with a guy who plays video games all day, smokes weed, or treats her terribly all because she feels she is no longer the priceless treasure she was meant to be.

I'm actually not against purity rings, but I worry about some of the messages that come with them. I told my Mackenzie, "I love that you want to go get this ring. And we will actually buy it for you because we are so proud that your desires match God's desires. But I want to make one thing clear. You can't actually lose your purity. You can lose your virginity, but you can't lose your purity. Your sins have been washed white as snow. How about we call it a 'pure heart' ring? Then you can focus on having a pure heart with God. When your thoughts are fixed on God, and your focus is on God, then your actions will follow."

Mackenzie loved this idea, and she is still wearing her pure heart ring. Teaching women this concept can help with preventing future unintended pregnancies by turning them toward a growing relationship with the God who loves them and has provided for their righteousness.

WHAT THE BIBLE HAS TO SAY
ABOUT PURE HEARTS

Romans 3:22 says, "This righteousness is given through faith in Jesus Christ to all who believe." What a promise and gift from God! Our actions don't dictate our purity. We are pure through the work of Jesus Christ alone.

We know that sex outside of marriage does not align with God's design. We know that sin has consequences that sometimes affect the rest of our lives. But using the phrase "lose your purity" can be misleading. When I say, I "lost my patience," I'm not making a forever-and-final statement about myself. I realize that I lost my patience in that moment. With God's help, I'll choose to exercise patience again the next day.

In the same way, a person who has been sexually active can choose to stay abstinent the next day. God's mercies are new every morning! We continually experience conviction about our actions that don't align with God's best for us, and we seek to bring those actions and attitudes under His authority in our lives, so that we can live like the loved and righteous children of God that He's made us to be. When we don't live according to who God says we are, the result can be a lifetime of hurt and pain.

His kindness leads us to repentance, and His goodness draws us to His side.

There are countless benefits to obeying God when it comes to sex outside of marriage and countless problems when we don't obey God. But this pattern is true of all sin, not just sexual sin.

The more we spend time with Jesus, the more our heart beats to the rhythm of our heavenly Father's. When we focus our thoughts on Him, that's when all of the "things we shouldn't be doing" become "things we don't want to do anymore." His kindness leads us to repentance, and His goodness draws us to His side.

I've had young women come up to me and ask, "My boyfriend and I are having sex. I'm not sure that God really minds since we already have a kid together. What do you think?"

I almost always respond with, "What do you think the Lord is saying to you about it?" Often she is unsure, so I encourage her to go spend quiet time with the Lord and just ask Him. I tell her to ask Him to highlight Scripture for her and give her peace about it. And then I invite her to come share with me later what she found.

Many young women don't ever come back to me about it on their own, although I know they looked. Maybe they just haven't figured out how to release that unhealthy soul tie that has been created. But some do come back to tell me what the Lord has shown them.

I get to say, "That is so amazing that you are hearing God speak to you! He loves you so much! Have you thought about how you will respond? Will you be obedient?"

For some women, it takes time before they can make the jump to stop. Some make the decision immediately. But by having them research and ask the Lord on their own instead of me just answering the question for them, they learn how to go to God for answers and how to commune with Him and they know that if they choose to be disobedient, they are disobeying God and not me (or some other church mentor). When she really begins to understand that God's law is our protection and not just a bunch of do's and don'ts, she begins to soften her heart and allow God to mold her into His image.

DISCOVERING YOUR PLACE

God's heart for marriage and family is important in the role of prevention. A lot of people were raised in a broken home. Few know what a healthy godly family even looks like. Some fathers indirectly teach their sons that women are just objects of pleasure, and some mothers indirectly teach their daughters that men are never to be respected. Inviting a new mom and her boyfriend into your life and into your home can show them what a family can look like—even the messy part.

Having a Christian family that follows God doesn't make us "good" or even worth being looked up to. We are not showing them what we have done. We are showing them how God makes dead people alive! They need to see that God loves ordinary people.

Once I heard a pastor tell how he and his wife were discipling another family. The family hangs out with them, and they share life together. One night, the pastor and his wife got into an argument in front of their guests.

The couple they were discipling felt awkward and said, "We're just going to go now and let you guys talk this out."

The pastor said, "No I need you to stay here and watch this fight because in a few minutes, you are going to see some healthy conflict resolution."

This is real life, and lessons are stronger when caught than when directly taught. The Message version translates what

Jesus said in Matthew 11:29–30: "Walk with me and work with me—watch how I do it. Learn the unforced rhythms of grace.... Keep company with me and you'll learn to live freely and lightly." Young moms and dads learn by seeing with their own eyes God's heart for family and marriage.

That is how we pave the way for pure hearts.

We can practice prevention strategies in the same way, by having hard conversations. We can teach that abstinence is *always* the best way to prevent an unplanned pregnancy. We can educate women about how our bodies work, how pregnancies happen, and when life begins. Let's face it, for most of us, science class is really boring in middle school and high school. This discussion is important and should be more than just a few days of curriculum presented by your science teacher!

> **Young moms and dads learn by seeing with their own eyes God's heart for family and marriage.**

I've met girls who are pregnant at fourteen and fifteen and just never realized what actually causes pregnancy. No one paved the way for their pure hearts. If we are willing to take the time and explain the science behind conception, young women will start to understand how God created them and that He holds the plan and purpose for their lives.

When you reach out to really know her, she will feel known by her heavenly Father, and will understand her value and the sacred quality of all life.

WHAT KNOWING HER CAN LOOK LIKE

There are great Bible-based sex education and abstinence programs available to help mentor one-on-one or teach in a large group or school. There are some that may not overtly talk about God but are written by believers and provide a good foundation to adapt to whatever opportunity arises. Make sure you research options so that you don't end up with a sex-education curriculum that doesn't line up with your beliefs.

I once visited a maternity home in Louisiana and toured one of their beautiful homes for homeless pregnant women. The house parents were a husband-and-wife team named Joe and Sandra, and they managed the day-to-day operations and helped the moms get back on their feet. They were amazing in their care for the moms.

Joe told me they'd housed some moms who had boyfriends, and there had to be strict rules about men coming in and out of the house. Joe would open certain times for visiting but his requirement was that each man who wanted to visit or date a pregnant mom living in the maternity home had to write Joe a letter of intent explaining why he wanted to date her and about his goals for the relationship. Joe said over the last eight years, only *one* man actually followed through and did this. The moms would quickly find out the man she thought was "the one" actually wasn't. She is worthy to be found and pursued by a godly man.

If a mom doesn't have a family that loves God and wants to protect her, then a mentor or mentor family can step into that role. She can write down what she hopes for in a future husband and pray for him before she even meets him or have her mentor family help her by asking him to write a letter of intent when she does begin to date.

My son Jess is twenty-one years old and just recently married the love of his life. Audrey and Jess had been dating for four years before marriage. When Jess approached Audrey's dad to ask permission to date his daughter, her dad spent a lot of time getting to know Jess. Then he agreed to let him date Audrey but wanted him to sign a contract first. You can read a copy of it below.

CONTRACT FOR A DATE WITH AUDREY

1. *I will stay active in my local church/youth group and will encourage Audrey to do the same.*

2. *I will clearly communicate the plans for the evening with Audrey's parents and will do my very best to follow those plans.*

3. *I will let Audrey's dad win any athletic contest.*

4. *I will not drink/use illegal drugs or entice others to do so. I will not allow anyone in my car to drink/use illegal drugs. I understand that drinking is illegal for people my age, and illegal drugs are illegal for everyone.*

5. *I will obey all traffic laws of this state and will take seriously the safety of Audrey, others, and myself.*

6. *I will safely strive to get Audrey home on time and will have Audrey call if we are going to be late. I understand that if I am late, I will come into Audrey's house and explain the reasons to Audrey's dad, even though he is probably going to be in bed.*

7. *Audrey is accustomed to being treated like a princess, and I will continue this tradition. If I have any questions about what treating Audrey like a princess means, I will ask Audrey's dad.*

8. *I will conduct myself in a pure and wholesome manner toward Audrey. If I have any questions about what it is to conduct myself in a pure and wholesome manner, I will ask Audrey's dad.*

9. *I will be a gentleman toward Audrey, her sister, and her parents. If I have any questions on what it is to be a gentleman, I will ask Audrey's dad.*

10. *I will open all doors for Audrey.*

11. *I understand that if I show disregard for this contract, it will likely be my last date with Audrey.*

Jess signed the contract. Four years later, and now they are married. Jess loves her so much and knows he has found a good and godly woman. What a gift for Audrey her father's love and protection have been! His character has given her a high standard for what she wants and expects in a husband.

Helping a single mom know her value and worth and helping her only date men who can see that too will pave the way for cultivating and preserving pure hearts. Showing her that you know she is a valued and valuable princess inspires abstinence and prevents unplanned pregnancies.

One of my favorite creative ways a church is helping unite families and prevent unplanned pregnancies is what my friends Bryan and Stephanie Carter, pastors of Concord Baptist Church in Dallas, Texas, are doing. They host a huge event every few years that usually makes the national news because it is so unique.

Bryan gave a call-to-arms in his church to disavow living together and commit to marriage. It was called the Step Into Marriage Challenge. Each couple begins the challenge with eleven weeks of pre-marital counseling that covers topics like finances, blended families, and sex. For the couple who makes it through all eleven weeks, Concord Church will sponsor a free wedding that includes a wedding dress, tuxedos, wedding bands, bouquets, and a wedding reception. All of the couples get married at the same ceremony at the same time.

To the couples that choose to bow out of the challenge, Pastor Carter will give one month's rent (up to $750) as long as it doesn't include a cohabitating partner. Bryan estimates that 80 percent of the fifty-seven couples he has married through mass ceremonies over the years have remained married. Concord Church has provided practical incentives to help couples choose a sexual life that honors God.

Many single moms who live with their boyfriend tell me they haven't gotten married yet because they really want a wedding and not just a trip to the courthouse. They want a dress and a beautiful wedding day. Concord Church found a great way to establish a foundation of commitment for couples and give these women the real wedding they hope for.

If you are not a pastor but you just know single parents who live together, coordinate and connect with people who might want to help them have a wedding ceremony! At Concord, local businesses donate gowns and tuxedos, and jewelers sell the rings to the church at a discount. Professional wedding planners, makeup artists, and hair stylists volunteer for the weddings. Be creative and get the word out! You never know who might want to contribute and be a part.

This challenge has now been adopted into six other churches around the nation. Bryan Carter said in a *New York Times* interview,[1] "Our hope was that this model was reproducible, because we hear from other churches that they need tools to help people build their families. We wanted it to be where we're not just talking about it and criticizing people. We wanted it to be, let's help them find a way to honor their relationship and honor God."

Men, your voice is important in the pro-life movement. This is not just a "women's issue." You not only have a voice in saving lives as you stand up for those who can't stand up for themselves, but your voice and presence can prevent unplanned pregnancies. When a woman knows what a godly husband looks like, she will have higher expectations for her future husband and dream about God's best for her.

I was visiting Embrace Grace leaders in another state one day, and they were telling me how their semester with their moms had been going. They spoke about the transformation they had seen in some of the moms over the course of just twelve weeks. They told about their Princess Day, which had just taken place the previous weekend.

One of their moms had been in and out of an abusive relationship for years. She had grown up in a home where there was no stability and not a lot of love. She dreamed about having a healthy family of her own someday.

Eventually this young woman met a man she thought might be her future husband, but he was verbally and emotionally abusive. She thought if she just worked on changing herself, then maybe he would stop. Finally she'd had enough. During her pregnancy, he had beaten her so thoroughly that she had lost all hearing in one of her ears. The Embrace Grace leaders rallied around her, supported her, and helped her get started with professional counseling. She stayed in the Embrace Grace classes and had her baby in the middle of the twelve-week semester, continuing to come even after the baby was born.

This young mom was there for Princess Day. At their event, the senior pastor of the church comes and helps serve a beautiful four-course dinner and prays over the women. At the end of the evening, each of the moms shared their favorite part of the semester. When they reached the sweet mom who had been abused, she said, "This moment right here. I know what I want for a future husband. I want a man like the pastor. I'm not saying I want *him*, of course. I've just never seen a man pray for someone else. My heart stirred when he did that. That's the kind of man I want leading my family. I want to wait for my future godly husband and not settle for anything until God helps him find me."

We hope a godly husband *will* find her because the example of a godly man has paved the way for him to get there. Whether she is called to marriage or a life of singleness, both are gifts from God. Marriage is a picture of God's relentless love and relationship with us. Singleness allows a life to fully devote time, focus, and energy to help others in the world in a way that married people can't. There is beauty and contentment found in both callings when a woman fully surrenders her life to be used for God's glory. She just has to look up and receive all that God has for her.

Ideas for How to Make Her Feel Known

- Help organize a health fair at a local school (with permission) and set up booths that address teen health, sexual health, and skills for healthy marriage that promote abstinence until marriage.

- The Friends-with-Benefits culture is prevalent with singles. Talk with a single mom you are mentoring about the beauty of sex and God's design for sex to be shared with one special person within the marriage relationship and why God planned it that way. Many women have never heard of abstinence until marriage as a way of life. Help her understand our God whose mercies are new every morning, and that she can start fresh today. It's never too late to abstain.

- Study sex education to help women and girls understand how ovulation is a sign of health. Getting certified will allow you to go into schools or other places to teach women how our miraculous bodies are designed. When women understand they were created and how reproduction works, they have the knowledge they need to make informed choices. You can get certified online through Femm Health.

- Become an accountability partner, as a single mom or mom-to-be commits to sexual abstinence. Help her set boundaries regarding what touching goes too far if she is in a situation with someone she likes, and encourage her to have the conversation with her boyfriend to get his agreement. Come up with ideas to prevent temptation and that will help her reach her goals, such as group dates, not being in a house alone with her boyfriend, or staying in the family's main living areas when hanging out with a date.

- If she struggles with going back to the same guy and then regretting sexual activity, there may be a soul tie that needs to be broken. Soul ties are spiritual and emotional connections with someone formed through a sexual relationship. Scripture talks about two becoming one flesh through marriage and sexual intimacy (Mark 10:8), and sexual partners are one way soul ties can be formed. Take her through an exercise of asking for forgiveness, getting rid of all items she has saved that still connect her to the unhealthy relationship, asking God to cancel any promises made to him, and then asking God to sever the soul tie. Be an accountability partner for her when she feels like she is having a weak moment and is tempted to go back to an unhealthy relationship.

- If she lives with her boyfriend and has a desire to get married but just doesn't have the funds for a wedding, check resources in your community that might help. Put the word out at bridal shops, florists, and bakeries. See if anyone wants to donate or offer a discount. Ask your church if she could have a wedding there for free.

- Write informative blog posts and articles that educate others about the importance of abstinence until marriage. Share with your social media following!

- Host a book club with single moms to read through books that inspire abstinence like *Unashamed* by Tracy Levinson and *Before He Finds You* by Ebony Wright, or *Sex and the Single Girl* by Juli Slattery. We can help each other by encouraging one another to stay focused on our long-term goals.

- Help her find tools that allow her to gain control over sexual thoughts and desires. Having these thoughts are totally normal, and she shouldn't feel guilty. But she can gain control over thoughts by turning on worship music, calling a friend, or staying busy during a weak moment. Help her talk out ways she can gain control when she feels tempted or if she needs to take her thoughts captive and set her mind on things above.

A National Ministry to Serve and Support

FEMM   FemmHealth.org

EMBRACE HER

Inviting Others to Join the Kingdom

My firstborn son, Jess, was the best gift ever. Nothing could have prepared me for that when I was a frightened nineteen-year-old with an unplanned pregnancy. Sometimes I laugh and say I may have raised that kid, but really he raised me too.

When my first book came out several years ago, I had to share my personal story again and again, often on large platforms or with national media. At times, it felt I was telling the whole world. There was only one problem with that.

I had never told Jess.

Ryan and I knew it was time. Jess was thirteen, and that's a tender age when kids are trying to find out who they are and why they are here. I laid the spiritual groundwork by having friends pray for us because I didn't want Jess to mistake my story as evidence that I didn't love him.

We went to the Cheesecake Factory, just Ryan, Jess, and me.

Ryan and I started by saying we were such young kids when we went to that abortion clinic thirteen years before. We had let fear consume us and convince us that abortion was the only thing that made sense. We didn't know what we needed, but God did.

We told Jess everything.

I couldn't read his blank expression when we finished, and I tried to get him to respond. Concerned, I asked, "How does this make you feel?"

"I dunno," he said.

We ended the evening without the healthy closure I had hoped for. But we didn't know what else we could say or do.

Over the next few months, Jess struggled with his identity. He started believing lies from Satan that he wasn't wanted or wasn't supposed to be here on earth.

I could see what was happening. The spiritual battle had heated up. Jess has an amazing call of God on his life, and it was obvious that the enemy doesn't want him to walk in that calling. I tried to think of ways to convince Jess that he is a mighty man of God with a holy purpose and plan. But words from a momma, as sweet as they are, do not compare to words from the heavenly Father.

One day, just about six months after we had told Jess our family story, the Lord spoke to his heart and changed everything. Jess was active in his youth group, and the youth pastor had asked him, "Jess, next week I want you to share for five minutes to all of the group about how you have overcome something in your life."

Jess had prayed about it, asking God what He wanted Jess to share. Just like that, God downloaded a triumphant message into Jess's heart that would preach victory, not only to the youth group, but to him as well.

A few days later, Jess came into my bedroom and said, "Mom, can I practice what I'm going to say at church?"

I couldn't say yes fast enough.

He began, "I was an overcomer before I was even born. Satan had a plan to take me out, but I'm here, and I'm going to use my life and story to change the world."

Needless to say, I was completely undone. You could see the change in his heart and his eyes. I was so proud of him as he got up on stage in front of hundreds in the youth group and shared his story of being an overcomer.

Jess is now twenty-one years old. He is passionate about making heaven crowded and has a desire to share the good news about Jesus with everyone he meets. He has introduced many kids to the Lord in just a short time and is now preaching and speaking on stages to whomever will listen. He is a world changer.

What if we lived in a world where it *always* made sense for a woman to have her baby, whether she placed for adoption or chose to parent?

Praise God that I never went back to that abortion clinic. I shudder to think what I had been considering. Now it's unthinkable.

Someone once told me that she had tried to explain to her ten-year-old son what an abortion is. She participated in a lot of pro-life work and wanted him to know the "why" behind her passion. As she spoke, his eyes widened.

Then he said, "Why would anyone not want to have their baby?"

The pro-life movement isn't just about saving a baby, it is about saving a whole lifetime.

To him, abortion was unthinkable. Can you imagine a world where everyone feels that way?

What if we lived in a world where it *always* made sense for a woman to have her baby, whether she placed for adoption or chose to parent? Imagine that every baby would have the opportunity to live and be valued from conception to their last day on earth.

Every person is God's masterpiece. Ephesians 2:10 promises, "For we are God's handiwork, created in Christ Jesus to do good works, which God prepared in advance for us to do." The pro-life movement isn't just about saving a baby, it is about saving a *whole lifetime*.

A true pro-life perspective requires a *pro-whole-life* approach that looks beyond the womb. Someone with a true pro-life perspective serves people from the "womb to the tomb."

Maybe you have a heart to care for the sick, those with disabilities, and the terminally ill.

Maybe your soul stirs for ministering to refugees and immigrants.

Maybe you have a passion to stand up against assisted suicide or the death penalty.

Maybe you feel a desire to care for the elderly as they pass from this earth to eternity.

Maybe what sets your soul on fire is to create plans that address health disparities and unemployment rates that impact the black community disproportionately or that correct education inequalities in underserved communities.

And maybe you haven't been dreaming of a huge service program. You just have been thinking about inviting your neighbor to church. That, my friend, is not too small a dream. Let's invite others to join the Kingdom. If the church is really the way that God changes the world, then the least we can do is help to make it bigger.

Courtney still loves being a part of her new church, well after graduating from the Embrace Grace class and having her baby. When she went to a pregnancy center during her unplanned pregnancy to hear about her options, she heard about Embrace Grace from the volunteers. Courtney then reached out via text to local leaders from three different churches that she found on our website. All three of the individual church leaders responded to the text, but one of them was diligent in continuing to pursue her.

She would invite Courtney to coffee and randomly send her worship songs to inspire and empower her. Those messages of hope always seemed to arrive at a moment she really needed them. Though Courtney wasn't choosing to connect with the church just yet, the leader kept encouraging her and would not let her stay isolated. She was persistent in inviting her to their group and loving her from afar.

And then Courtney *was* ready.

Even though this church was twice as far as the other two churches Courtney had considered—more than thirty miles from her home, to be exact—that was the Embrace Grace group she ultimately chose to attend. As she came to the class weekly, she fell more and more in love with the people and found a place where she knew she belonged.

Courtney has now completed the program and leads the very group that poured into her for over a year. She also volunteers at the church during the weekend services. She doesn't mind the drive because she has found her church family and a way to serve in the Kingdom of God.

By pursuing Courtney, that church leader proved that the church loved her before they even met her. They welcomed her as their own. They checked on her when she missed a class. They bought her a bed when they heard she was sleeping on the floor. They poured care and attention into her kids, and now her kids love coming to church several times a week. These believers knew the church is where Courtney belonged.

The church is the hope of the world, and we are better together. It will take all of us to change the way things are.

If we truly believe God wants every human being to be a son or daughter of the King whose rightful place is in His Kingdom, we must keep inviting them to walk through the doors . . . of *home*.

WHAT THE BIBLE HAS TO SAY ABOUT JOINING THE KINGDOM

We are all on the same team. Building the Kingdom of God is a *team* sport. The apostle Paul explains, "Neither the one who plants nor the one who waters is anything, but only God, who makes things grow. . . . For we are co-workers in God's service" (1 Cor. 3:7, 9). Did you catch that? We are *all* God's servants in

His Kingdom, and we all have a mission that God downloads to us daily. We just have to hear, believe, and obey. We can cheer on our new brothers and sisters in Christ because when one of us is serving well, we all win.

The church is the hope of the world, and we are better together. It will take all of us, using our gifts and strengths, with our individual stories and passions as our fuel, to change the way things are. If you still feel stuck or unsure where to start reaching out, a simple way to begin is to spend some time with people who are already in your congregation but aren't in the same life station as you.

Somewhere, a twelve-year-old is looking for a mentor.

Somewhere, the flustered mom of a toddler is looking for a helping hand.

Somewhere, a lonely widow is looking for a kind visitor.

God sees you, and He sees the person in need. All you have to do is ask Him to connect you.

DISCOVERING YOUR PLACE

Pastor Rick Warren said, "A thousand years from today, if there's still Earth here, there won't be a Microsoft. There won't be a Hollywood a thousand years from today. There won't be a United States of America, because no earthly kingdom lasts forever. There won't be all of the things we think are so great, but there will still be the family of God. God's people last. It's the only thing that's going to last. . . . I make no apology in saying to you that maybe joining a spiritual family will be the most significant thing you do with your life."[1]

Do you agree that "joining a spiritual family is the most significant thing" a person can do? If so, why are we hesitant to offer this incredible opportunity to others? Your life-changing impact could start with something as simple as an invitation to join you at church.

I've met many people who have a passion to start a ministry but stop too soon. They think it would cost a lot of money they don't have. So they just put the dream on the shelf and keep going with life as it was before they had the dream. Is that the best response? Is it reasonable to think, "If I can't serve in a big way, then I might as well not serve at all"?

Why do we think we have to know what steps 2, 10, or 500 are before we take step 1? It doesn't usually happen that way because faith isn't a feeling based on steps we can see. It is a choice to trust that God will lead you to the next right step when you get there. Faith is taking many "Step 1s," one after another.

Sure, you might be waiting on God to fulfill your dream. But at the same time, He might be prompting you to step out to begin, in faith.

WHAT EMBRACING HER CAN LOOK LIKE

At the Embrace Grace baby showers, every new mom receives a Bible as one of her gifts. A lot of the moms are brand-new in their relationship with God and do not know where to start in studying God's Word. I have seen churches take that Bible and pass it around before the big day, spending a few weeks with group leaders highlighting their favorite verses, writing encouraging notes in the margins, and putting bookmarks in favorite passages. This helps the young mom know where to start, and she feels so loved and empowered receiving a beautiful gift that her new church family spent time on just for her. Is there anything a single mother could need more than to read truth everyday? The Bible will tell her who she is and remind her that God loves her. Giving a beautifully prepared Bible is a great way to love single moms, dads, and even children. You and your friends can purchase Bibles and mark them up to help guide a new believer.

The Loved Bible Project is an organization doing this very thing. They believe it blesses the giver and the receiver to mark beloved passages in a Bible and offer it as a gift. As the giver searches God's Word to highlight how it can encourage, comfort, and give hope to someone, they have the opportunity to stop and be amazed by God and His grace all over again. And for the receiver, a Loved Bible is a present full of promises they might have had a hard time finding on their own. The highlighting and margin notes provide a head start so she doesn't feel she has so much catching up to do.

The message communicated when a church fully embraces a single mother is profound. It is a way of saying, *You are part of the church now. We love you. We need you. You belong here in the Kingdom. You weren't just our project, and we don't look down on you as if you are beneath us. We see you eye-to-eye. We serve with you hand-in-hand. We are your brothers and sisters, and we're not just family for you now.*

We're yours forever.

Sitting across the table from the pastor of a church, I couldn't hold back my happy tears. He had been sharing about his daughter Abby having an unplanned pregnancy and the effect it had, not only on his family, but also on the church that he pastored.

The father of the baby was in and out of jail and not a part of her life, and Abby had asked for forgiveness. She wanted to come back home. Eventually, Abby gave birth to a sweet baby girl. Everyone in the family was happy about this new addition, even though the timing wasn't what they had hoped.

During the pregnancy, the pastor had shared the news with his congregation, and it was received with grace. Members of the church had purchased gifts for the baby, dropping them on their doorstep. They would encourage Abby and thank her for choosing life.

Then what he said next touched me deeply.

The pastor told me that Abby asked him if it would be okay to dedicate her baby, his grandchild, at his church. He agreed, and they arranged for the baby dedication at their next scheduled ceremonies. At their baby dedication ceremony, when each family walks to the altar, the pastor will ask, "Would the family members who represent this child please stand?"

That's when all family members connected to that baby will stand. Then the pastor leads a prayer of dedication for that specific family.

On the night when Abby signed up for her baby dedication, family after family took their turns at the altar, until finally, it was her turn.

The pastor asked the same question he had asked with each

of the other families, "Would the family members who represent this woman and her child please stand?"

What happened next is the perfect picture of God's dream for the world:

The whole church stood up.

Ideas for How to Embrace Her

- Buy her a Bible. Help her know where to start by highlighting verses, writing on sticky notes, cards, sheets of paper. Encourage her in the margins. Include prayers and songs that will inspire and bless.

- Start a Bible reading plan with her. Hold each other accountable. Check out a great reading plan through the Bible Recap podcast. You can download the audio or print their plan for Bible reading, and then listen to the Bible Recap podcast to go over highlights of what you just learned. Be relaxed with it, and even if the young mom only has time to listen to the recap, that's okay. New moms have a lot on their plate. There's no place for guilt-trips because God doesn't use guilt to motivate us in relationship with Him. He is patient and kind.

- When you're buying a devotional or new spiritual book for yourself, grab an extra one for her.

- Disciple her—and eventually teach her how to make disciples.

- Cover the cost for her to attend a women's ministry retreat. Babysit or arrange for reliable childcare so she can go and fully focus on what God wants to speak to her.

- Buy an extra ticket to that women's conference coming up and bring her along with you!

- Find special classes or Bible studies within your church that are teaching subjects that would directly minister to her.

- Send her your favorite worship songs and tell her why it ministers to you.

- Connect her to your favorite podcasts for spiritual development.

- Tell her about your favorite pastors who have services broadcast online for times when she can't make it on a Sunday to your church, so she can still be ministered to at home.

- Ask her to make a wish list of goals she has for growing her spiritual roots. Maybe she would like to memorize Scripture or deep-dive study a specific book of the Bible. Get her pointing in the right direction to reach her goal.

- Ask her when she is most relaxed, what is she doing? Is she going for a walk? Taking a nap? Reading a book? Offer to babysit for thirty minutes or an hour so she can get a little of that a few times each week.

- Buy her a gratitude journal—or just buy any journal and call it a gratitude journal. Inspire her to write in it every day so she can get into the practice of being grateful for how God is all that she needs.

- Find out when your church has an upcoming baby dedication service and ask if she would like to dedicate her baby in the Lord and share what that means. Take her shopping for a new outfit for her and her baby so she feels special on such an amazing occasion.

- Teach her to listen for God's voice. Start with simple ways like having her write a letter to God and then write a letter of what she feels God would say back to her. Read over and make sure it all aligns with God's Word. Be a safe person to process with when she feels the Holy Spirit may be speaking to her.

- Share your personal struggles and what the Lord is speaking to you through it. Be vulnerable and authentic. She needs you to be real with her.

- Teach her how to share her testimony with someone if she only had one minute. Then teach her how she might share if she had five minutes. Weed out details that are not as important to the big picture of what God has done. Encourage her, and pray together that God would give her an opportunity to share her testimony.

- Encourage worship through drama, video, art, and music, and show her the many creative ways we can worship our Creator.

- Have her take her spiritual gifts test. Go over the results and dig into the Scriptures that connect to that gift. Find ways for her to practice her gifts and serve others.

- Talk with church leadership about an upcoming opportunity for people to be baptized, and ask her if she would like to be baptized.

- Teach her how to pray!

- Help her find opportunities to serve others. She may even want to choose some of the helping suggestions listed in this book.

National Organizations That Support and Serve

Bible Recap	thebiblerecap.com
Loved Bible Project	lovedbibleproject.com
Mardel Bookstore	mardel.com
Spiritual gifts test	giftstest.com

BEAUTY FOR ASHES

Have you ever had a dream while you were awake? Not a daydream, which seems more fun and frivolous, but a dream that captured your whole attention and really stayed with you?

It happened to me, right during a time of worship at a women's conference at my home church, Gateway. My waking dream felt as if I were viewing a photo reel of memories in my mind. The series began with an image of me as a teenager, consumed with fear because of what I'd just learned: I was pregnant. The scenes were dark. I was nervous and alone.

But then those darker, sadder photos were suddenly replaced with mental snapshots of recent, joyful memories, where I was smiling, happily hosting baby showers. This made sense, as I had thrown thirteen baby showers in the past year. My girlfriends had a lot of babies that year! As those first frightened images from my past turned into bright and cheerful scenes, the mental photo reel underwent a beautiful transformation.

All those images flew through my mind in just a few seconds, as worship continued around me. I knew, though, that my waking dream held significance. Right away, I prayed and asked God what it might mean.

As the service came to a close and women were leaving, I caught up with the women's ministries pastor. I told her about my experience of the visual memories of my teen pregnancy linked with happy memories of recent baby shower celebrations. She didn't even hesitate but instantly suggested, "Why don't you start a small group for women with unplanned pregnancies? You could plan a baby shower as a draw to get them in the door."

And that's how God began a ministry—a ministry to me and other leaders of Embrace Grace, a ministry to so many young mothers who were pregnant and alone. As my pastor, Robert Morris, describes it, "Embrace Grace now has over 716 active support groups in 655 churches across 47 states and 10 countries. They've partnered with 567 pregnancy centers to change the lives of the next generation in their time of greatest need. More than 2,670 leaders have helped lead groups, throw baby showers, and pamper the girls on Princess Days. And best of all, more than 6,000 women have chosen life for their babies, while being empowered to have hope and encouraged in their walk with the Lord."

This is what God does when His people come together to help others be brave, relinquishing fears to receive from God something so much better! Isaiah 61 describes how God, by His Spirit, uses people to "proclaim good news," "bind up the brokenhearted," and "proclaim freedom." And God's ultimate purpose?

To bestow on them a crown of beauty
    instead of ashes,
the oil of joy
    instead of mourning,
and a garment of praise
    instead of a spirit of despair.

God is at work, in love drawing people into His family. You can be part of His work by showing His love to pregnant women and single mothers. Start with one, and jump right in to helping her be brave.

ACKNOWLEDGMENTS

I am surrounded by amazing people who encourage, inspire, support, and believe in me. I feel like one of the most blessed women in the world! This book would not be a reality if it weren't for them.

To my husband: Ryan Ford. You have chosen me for more than twenty-five years now, and there is no one else in the world I would rather be doing this crazy life with. Thank you for adjusting your schedule to make time for me to write this book.

To my kids and bonus kid: Jess, Audrey, Mackenzie, Landry, and Judah Brave. You all are my favorite humans on this planet. You are a gift from heaven and a joy to spend time with. Even though we were quarantined and going through a crazy pandemic, you gave me space and time to get this book knocked out.

To our Embrace Grace Dream Team: Morgan, Megan, Alyssa, Jennifer, Madeline, Melissa, Shelby, Jessica, Lauren, Susan, Monica, Wendi, Kaitlyn, Aidan, Ryan, and Bob. You make us look good. Thank you for being revivalists, creating a culture of honor and excellence, leading authentic lives as true wonder-seekers, and having audacious love. You are the best example of what pro-love looks like. It is an honor to serve with you.

To Nika Maples: You are the best book coach anyone could ever have. Thank you for helping me conceive this big dream and break it down into manageable pieces so I could get this book done! Thank you for crying with me as we talked through the glory stories throughout. I could not have written this book without you!

To my agent: Rachel Kent. Thank you for believing in this book and representing me so well. I'm so thankful for you!

To the Moody team: editors Judy and Annette, and the amazing marketing team. Thank you for saying yes. It has been a joy partnering with you on this book. Your passion for life is contagious, and I know all your hard work with this book will help save many lives!

To all my pro-life friends working in the movement: There are way too many of you to list here. You know who you are. Thank you for desiring unity and cheering on our fellow pro-life organizations. We all need each other. "Let us not become weary in doing good, for at the proper time we will reap a harvest if we do not give up" (Gal. 6:9).

To my pastors Robert and Debbie Morris, and my Gateway Church family: Thank you for being our spiritual covering and believing in Embrace Grace. The effects of your prayers and support has created a national impact and thousands of lives saved both physically and eternally. I would never have been able to write this book if I had not had a safe place to call home.

NOTES

INTRODUCTION

1. "Unmarried Childbearing," Centers for Disease Control and Prevention, November 27, 2019, https://www.cdc.gov/nchs/fastats/unmarried-childbearing.htm.
2. "Induced Abortion in the United States," Guttmacher Institute, September 2019, https://www.guttmacher.org/fact-sheet/induced-abortion-united-states.
3. "Abortion Surveillance—United States, 2013," Centers for Disease Control and Prevention, November 25, 2016, https://www.cdc.gov/mmwr/volumes/65/ss/ss6512a1.htm.
4. Lisa Cannon Green, "New Survey: Women Go Silently from Church to Abortion Clinic," Care Net, November 23, 2015, https://www.care-net.org/churches-blog/new-survey-women-go-silently-from-church-to-abortion-clinic.
5. "The Majority of Children Live with Two Parents, Census Bureau Reports," United States Census Bureau, November 17, 2016, https://www.census.gov/newsroom/press-releases/2016/cb16-192.html.

6. Lawrence B. Finer et al.,"Reasons U.S. Women Have Abortions: Quantitative and Qualitative Perspectives," *Perspectives on Sexual and Reproductive Health* 37, no. 3 (2005): 110–18, https://www.guttmacher.org/journals/psrh/2005/reasons-us-women-have-abortions-quantitative-and-qualitative-perspectives.
7. Destiny Herndon-de la Rosa, "I Didn't Have an Abortion, and It Saved My Life . . .," *New Wave Feminists*, March 4, 2016, http://newwavefeminists.blogspot.com/2016/03/i-didnt-have-abortion-and-it-saved-my.html?m=0.

CHAPTER 2: COMFORT HER

1. Thomas A. Glessner, "National Survey of Pro-Life Pregnancy Centers Shows Major Influence of Ultrasound on a Mother's Choice for Life," *Christian Newswire*, March 3, 2015, http://www.christiannewswire.com/news/7390775641.html.
2. "Option Ultrasound Program," Focus on the Family, accessed June 20, 2020, https://www.focusonthefamily.com/pro-life/option-ultrasound-program-2/.

CHAPTER 3: WELCOME HER

1. Max Lucado (@MaxLucado), Twitter, January 17, 2011, 9:19 a.m., https://twitter.com/maxlucado/status/27022300356284416?lang=en.

CHAPTER 4: PROTECT HER

1. "Hobby Lobby Supreme Court Case," Hobby Lobby Newsroom, accessed June 23, 2020, https://newsroom.hobbylobby.com/hobby-lobby-case/.

2. "Supreme Court Issues Decision on HHS Mandate Case," Little Sisters of the Poor, May 16, 2016, http://littlesistersofthepoor .org/events/supreme-court-issues-decision-on-hhs-mandate-case/.

CHAPTER 6: SUPPORT HER

1. Erin Dunbar, "Free Haircut Event for Kids in Foster, Adoptive and Kinship Families at Paul Mitchell School," WHNT 19 News, September 9, 2019, https://whnt.com/news/huntsville/ free-haircut-event-for-kids-in-foster-adoptive-and-kinship-families-at-paul-mitchell-school/.
2. "Discounts and Special Offers for Foster Families," Still Orphans, May 4, 2018, https://www.stillorphans.com/2018/05/04/ discounts-and-special-offers-for-foster-families/.

CHAPTER 7: FREE HER

1. Joy Eggerichs, "Christine Caine: Christians Should Be the 'Most Relationally Functional' People on Earth," *Relevant Magazine,* August 28, 2018, https://relevantmagazine.com/ culture/books/qa-christine-caine/.
2. Abby Johnson, quoted in "Pastors – We Need You!," Central Texas Coalition for Life, accessed June 23, 2020, https://www .centraltexascoalition.com/for-pastors/.

CHAPTER 8: EMPOWER HER

1. "National Snapshot: Poverty among Women & Families, 2019," National Women's Law Center, October 23, 2019, https:// nwlc.org/resources/national-snapshot-poverty-among-women-families-2019/.

2. "2019 Poverty Guidelines," ASPE, accessed June 23, 2020, https://aspe.hhs.gov/2019-poverty-guidelines.

3. "Abortion Surveillance—United States, 2016," Centers for Disease Control and Prevention, November 29, 2019, https://www.cdc.gov/mmwr/volumes/68/ss/ss6811a1.htm.

CHAPTER 9: KNOW HER

1. Tammy La Gorce, "Dallas Megachurch Offers Free Weddings for Couples Living Together, on One Condition," *New York Times*, July 11, 2019, https://www.nytimes.com/2019/07/11/fashion/weddings/dallas-mass-wedding-after-taking-marriage-challenge.html.

CHAPTER 10: EMBRACE HER

1. Rick Warren, quoted in Michael Gryboski, "Rick Warren: 'Family of God' Will Outlast Microsoft, Hollywood, the United States," *Christian Post*, July 1, 2016, https://www.christianpost.com/news/rick-warren-family-of-god-will-outlast-microsoft-hollywood-united-states.html.